TAKE A WALK
PORTLAND

TAKE A WALK
PORTLAND

———

*More Than 75 Walks in Natural Places from the
Gorge to Hillsboro and Vancouver to Tualatin*

Brian Barker

SASQUATCH BOOKS
SEATTLE

To Elizabeth and Ben—may we always walk our paths together

Printed in the United States of America

Published by Sasquatch Books

21 20 19 18 17   9 8 7 6 5 4 3 2 1

Editor: Gary Luke
Production editor: Em Gale
Cover design: Mikko Kim
Interior design: Bryce de Flamand
Cover photograph: Brian Barker
Interior photographs: Brian Barker
Maps: Lisa Brower
Copyeditor: Janice Lee

Library of Congress Cataloging-in-Publication Data is available.

ISBN: 978-1-63217-088-0

Sasquatch Books
1904 Third Avenue, Suite 710
Seattle, WA 98101
(206) 467-4300
www.sasquatchbooks.com
custserv@sasquatchbooks.com

Certified Chain of Custody
Promoting Sustainable Forestry
www.sfiprogram.org
SFI-01268

SUSTAINABLE FORESTRY INITIATIVE

SFI label applies to the text stock

CONTENTS

WALKS AT A GLANCE

Walk #	Trail/Park	Park Acreage	Miles of Trail	Connecting Trails	ADA Trail*	Dogs**	Bicycles**	Horses**
SOUTHWEST PORTLAND								
1	Hoyt Arboretum	187	12	✓	✓	✓		
2	4T Trail	n/a	4.5	✓		✓		
3	Marquam Nature Park	176	1.6	✓		✓		
4	Terwilliger Parkway	99	5	✓	✓	✓		
5	Gabriel Park	90	3		✓	✓		
6	Marshall Park	26	2			✓		
7	Woods Memorial Natural Area	36	1.5			✓		
8	Maricara Natural Area	17	1	✓		✓		
9	River View Natural Area	146	2.5			✓		
10	Tryon Creek State Natural Area	658	8		✓	✓		✓
NORTHWEST PORTLAND & FOREST PARK								
11	Lower Macleay Park to Pittock Mansion	5,172	2.5	✓	✓	✓		
12	Audubon Society of Portland Pittock Bird Sanctuary	30	1.3	✓				
13	Audubon Society of Portland Collins and Uhtoff Sanctuaries	120	1.3	✓				

n/a	Information not available, particularly concerning acreage of land surrounding converted railway trails
ADA Trail*	Sometimes only one trail or segments of a trail will be ADA compliant
**	May or may not be permitted on all trails
OL	Off-leash area in, or connected to, park/trail
NB	No bicycles

Restrooms	Picnic Areas	Playground	Freshwater Beach	Forest	Stream/River/Creek	Wetlands/Marsh	Lake	Meadow/Farmland	Mountain Views	Interpretive Center	Best Birding	Gardens	Sports Facilities	Campgrounds	Historical Site
✓	✓			✓					✓	✓		✓			
				✓					✓						
	✓			✓											
	✓			✓					✓			✓			
✓				✓	✓								✓		
	✓	✓		✓	✓										
				✓	✓	✓									
				✓	✓										
				✓							✓				
✓				✓	✓					✓	✓				
✓				✓	✓				✓	✓					✓
✓				✓	✓				✓	✓					
✓				✓					✓	✓					

Walk #	Trail/Park	Park Acreage	Miles of Trail	Connecting Trails	ADA Trail*	Dogs**	Bicycles**	Horses**
14	Forest Park Nature Trail Loop	5,172	3	✓		✓	✓	
15	Forest Park Firelane 15 Loop	5,172	4.2	✓		✓	✓	

NORTH PORTLAND & SAUVIE ISLAND

Walk #	Trail/Park	Park Acreage	Miles of Trail	Connecting Trails	ADA Trail*	Dogs**	Bicycles**	Horses**
16	Smith and Bybee Wetlands Natural Area	2,000	1	✓	✓			
17	Columbia Slough Trail	n/a	4		✓	✓	✓	
18	Kelley Point Park	104	2	✓	✓	✓	✓	
19	Wapato Access Greenway State Park Trail	15	2			✓		✓
20	Oak Island Trail	n/a	2.4			✓		
21	Warrior Rock Lighthouse Trail	n/a	3.2			✓		
22	Crown Zellerbach Trail	n/a	22		✓	✓	✓	✓

SOUTHEAST PORTLAND

Walk #	Trail/Park	Park Acreage	Miles of Trail	Connecting Trails	ADA Trail*	Dogs**	Bicycles**	Horses**
23	Oaks Bottom Wildlife Refuge	141	2.4	✓		✓	✓	
24	Crystal Springs Rhododendron Garden	7	1	✓	✓	✓		
25	Reed College Canyon	15	1	✓		✓		
26	Lone Fir Cemetery	30	1		✓			
27	Mount Tabor Park	191	9		✓	✓	✓	

EAST PORTLAND & GRESHAM

Walk #	Trail/Park	Park Acreage	Miles of Trail	Connecting Trails	ADA Trail*	Dogs**	Bicycles**	Horses**
28	Glendoveer Fitness Trail	242	2.2					
29	Powell Butte Nature Park	611	8	✓	✓	✓	✓	✓
30	Butler Creek Greenway Trail	40	1.4	✓	✓	✓	✓	
31	Gresham Butte Saddle Trail	850	1.2	✓		✓	✓	
32	Oxbow Regional Park	1,000	12		✓			✓
33	Scouters Mountain Nature Park	100	1.2		✓			

Restrooms	Picnic Areas	Playground	Freshwater Beach	Forest	Stream/River/Creek	Wetlands/Marsh	Lake	Meadow/Farmland	Mountain Views	Interpretive Center	Best Birding	Gardens	Sports Facilities	Campgrounds	Historical Site
				✓											
				✓	✓			✓							
✓						✓				✓					
					✓	✓			✓	✓					
✓	✓		✓	✓	✓			✓	✓	✓	✓				
	✓			✓			✓				✓				
✓				✓		✓	✓		✓		✓				
✓			✓	✓	✓				✓		✓				
				✓							✓				
				✓		✓		✓			✓				
✓							✓			✓	✓	✓			
					✓	✓	✓				✓				
											✓				✓
✓		✓		✓					✓		✓				
✓											✓				
✓				✓		✓		✓	✓	✓	✓				
				✓	✓						✓				
				✓							✓				
✓	✓							✓			✓			✓	
✓	✓			✓					✓						

VANCOUVER, WASHINGTON

Walk #	Trail/Park	Park Acreage	Miles of Trail	Connecting Trails	ADA Trail*	Dogs**	Bicycles**	Horses**
34	Salmon Creek Greenway Trail	403	3.1	✓	✓	✓	✓	✓
35	Burnt Bridge Creek Greenway Trail	185	1.5	✓	✓	✓	✓	
36	Frenchman's Bar Trail	120	3	✓	✓	✓	✓	
37	Columbia Springs	100	2	✓		✓		
38	Ridgefield National Wildlife Refuge Oaks to Wetlands Trail	5,218	2		✓			
39	Ridgefield National Wildlife Refuge Kiwa Trail	5,218	1.5		✓			
40	Lewisville Regional Park	154	2.5		✓	✓	✓	
41	Battle Ground Lake State Park	280	10			✓	✓	✓
42	La Center Bottoms	314	2		✓	✓		✓

SOUTHWEST WASHINGTON

Walk #	Trail/Park	Park Acreage	Miles of Trail	Connecting Trails	ADA Trail*	Dogs**	Bicycles**	Horses**
43	Lacamas Lake Regional Park	312	6	✓		✓	✓	
44	Lacamas Heritage Trail	n/a	3.5	✓	✓	✓	✓	
45	Columbia River Dike Trail	n/a	4	✓	✓	✓	✓	✓
46	Gibbons Creek Wildlife Art Trail	1,049	2.75	✓	✓			

COLUMBIA RIVER GORGE

Walk #	Trail/Park	Park Acreage	Miles of Trail	Connecting Trails	ADA Trail*	Dogs**	Bicycles**	Horses**
47	Sandy River Delta	1,400	1.3		✓	✓	✓	✓
48	Rooster Rock State Park	872	3			✓		
49	Bridal Veil Falls	15	1.2		✓	✓		
50	Latourell Falls	378	2.3		✓	✓		
51	Historic Columbia River Highway State Trail (Tooth Rock)	259	2	✓	✓	✓	✓	
52	Strawberry Island	45	3			✓		
53	Fort Cascades Loop	n/a	1.5		✓	✓		
54	Sams Walker Nature Trail	65	1.1		✓	✓		

Restrooms	Picnic Areas	Playground	Freshwater Beach	Forest	Stream/River/Creek	Wetlands/Marsh	Lake	Meadow/Farmland	Mountain Views	Interpretive Center	Best Birding	Gardens	Sports Facilities	Campgrounds	Historical Site
✓		✓		✓	✓	✓			✓		✓		✓		
✓				✓	✓	✓					✓				
✓	✓		✓	✓	✓						✓		✓		
✓				✓							✓				
✓				✓		✓				✓	✓				
				✓		✓					✓				
✓	✓			✓	✓	✓							✓		
✓	✓			✓			✓							✓	
✓					✓	✓					✓				
✓		✓		✓			✓			✓					
✓				✓			✓			✓	✓				
✓	✓		✓	✓	✓	✓			✓		✓				✓
✓						✓			✓		✓				
✓				✓	✓	✓					✓				
✓	✓		✓	✓	✓									✓	✓
✓				✓											✓
✓				✓											✓
✓				✓	✓										✓
				✓	✓				✓		✓				
✓				✓	✓					✓					✓
✓				✓	✓	✓		✓	✓		✓				✓

Walk #	Trail/Park	Park Acreage	Miles of Trail	Connecting Trails	ADA Trail*	Dogs**	Bicycles**	Horses**
CLACKAMAS COUNTY								
55	George Rogers Park	26	1.3		✓	✓	✓	
56	Iron Mountain Park	51	1.5			✓		✓
57	Bryant Woods Nature Park	17	1.6	✓	✓	✓		
58	Cooks Butte Park	42	2	✓		✓	✓	
59	Stafford Basin Trail at Luscher Farm	154	2.4		✓	✓	✓	
60	Mary S. Young State Park	133	1		✓	✓		
61	Wilderness Park	51	1.5			✓		
62	Mount Talbert Nature Park	216	4		✓			
63	Camassia Natural Area	26	1					
64	Canemah Bluff Nature Park	271	1.2		✓			
65	Hopkins Demonstration Forest	140	5			✓		
66	Cazadero Trail	n/a	3		✓	✓	✓	
67	Milo McIver Bat Trail	950	1			✓		✓
WASHINGTON COUNTY								
68	Fanno Creek Greenway Trail	87	1.8		✓	✓	✓	
69	Tualatin Hills Nature Park	222	5	✓	✓		✓	
70	Tualatin River National Wildlife Refuge	1,800	1		✓			
71	Cooper Mountain Nature Park	230	3		✓			
72	Brown's Ferry Park	28	2.2	✓	✓	✓		
73	Graham Oaks Nature Park	250	3	✓	✓	✓	✓	
74	Jackson Bottom Wetlands Preserve	725	4.5					
75	Fernhill Wetlands	700	1.1		✓			
76	Banks-Vernonia State Trail	n/a	21	✓	✓	✓	✓	✓
77	Champoeg State Heritage Area	615	3.9		✓	✓	✓	

Restrooms	Picnic Areas	Playground	Freshwater Beach	Forest	Stream/River/Creek	Wetlands/Marsh	Lake	Meadow/Farmland	Mountain Views	Interpretive Center	Best Birding	Gardens	Sports Facilities	Campgrounds	Historical Site
✓	✓				✓								✓		
				✓											
				✓	✓			✓			✓				
				✓				✓			✓				
✓						✓		✓			✓				✓
✓	✓			✓	✓						✓		✓		
				✓							✓				
✓	✓			✓							✓				
							✓	✓	✓		✓				
✓		✓		✓				✓			✓		✓		✓
✓				✓	✓	✓				✓					
				✓	✓										
✓				✓				✓	✓				✓	✓	
		✓			✓	✓					✓		✓		
✓				✓		✓				✓	✓				
✓				✓	✓	✓				✓	✓				
✓		✓		✓							✓	✓			
✓				✓	✓						✓				✓
✓	✓			✓		✓					✓				
					✓	✓				✓	✓				
✓	✓					✓			✓		✓	✓			
✓	✓			✓	✓										✓
✓				✓	✓						✓		✓	✓	✓

INTRODUCTION

My first nature walks took place in Kirby Creek, a small forest in suburban Grand Prairie, Texas. There I'd roam for hours, accompanied by my brother. We ate wild grapes; poked at crayfish; got stung by fire ants, wasps, and scorpions; built forts; swung on ropes; and generally learned to fend for ourselves. My love of nature was truly born in those woods. It's a love I've kept but experienced in other, faster ways since then: skiing, biking, and huffing up remote mountains, always racing to the summit. I've learned to slow down now (having a son will do that to you) and to appreciate nature wherever I find it, at a pace that allows the details to burrow in. And I really believe there's no better place for that than in Portland, where it feels something akin to living in an arboretum. World-class parks, ancient forests, bird-rich wetlands, big rivers, and Cascade Range views are all within easy reach of town. And once you arrive, there's no better way to enjoy them than with a good walk.

How These Walks Were Chosen

These seventy-seven walks lie within the Portland metro area, extending to the Columbia River Gorge, both sides of the Columbia River, and the foothills of the Oregon Coast Range mountains. Except for occasional seasonal wildlife closures, these walks are all accessible year-round. Most are child- and dog-friendly and are easy, short walks just minutes from your home or workplace, be it in Portland, Beaverton, Vancouver, Lake Oswego, or any of the communities in between. All these destinations can be reached inside of an hour, and most are less than 45 miles or 45 minutes away (assuming you're not stuck in Portland's increasingly common traffic jams).

Most of the walks in this book offer more than a mile of walking and are in parks or natural settings. Walking these paths requires no special equipment other than a good pair of walking shoes (and, since this is Portland, a rain jacket is always a good idea). Most travel over gentle or moderate terrain; we'll leave the long, sustained climbs to the hikers. Outings that happen to fall short on mileage or require a more strenuous effort in some sections offer rich rewards to compensate, be it significant beauty, unique cultural heritage, or both. Most are also a short drive (or walk) from other trails or parks where you can easily extend your outing.

Keeping Updated

I walk trails in town regularly, and I walked every path found in this book in the spring of 2016—in some cases, many times. And while I tried to be as comprehensive as possible, when this book was going to press, new natural areas were in the works from north of Forest Park in the Tualatin Mountains to the Chehalem Mountains in Forest Grove. Established trails are also constantly being expanded, repaired, and temporarily closed or detoured. And gaps in greenway and commuter trails are being filled, with even more grand plans on the way. What a wonderful problem to have!

Because of this constant growth and change, things may not be as I have portrayed them by the time you take some of these walks. With luck, the changes will be for the better.

Thoughts on Safety

Not every trail is as safe as a suburban sidewalk. Despite maintenance efforts, mudslides obliterate paths, rain erodes them, and fallen trees block them. Walking in natural places can be risky. Wear appropriate footwear and try to walk with someone else, especially in the more remote parks. Be aware that wildlife, such as mountain lions, coyotes, and bears, are often present in parks, but are rarely seen on trails. Take common sense, a smartphone, and anything else you'll need. Tell someone where you're going and when you expect to be back. You're on your own.

Trails and Parks Belong to Everyone

My experience is that most people who share trails respect the natural areas and understand the need for preservation and care. But whether parks are signposted or not, the same minimal courtesies are asked of all visitors:

1. Stay on the trail.
2. Keep pets on a leash unless in a designated off-leash area. Always clean up after your dog.
3. Keep children and pets out of salmon-spawning creeks.
4. Don't feed the waterfowl, squirrels, or other wildlife.
5. Don't pick the flowers or forage for mushrooms.
6. Take only memories and pictures. Leave only footprints.

With everyone's cooperation, we can preserve our trails for ourselves and as a heritage for generations to come.

Consider Volunteering

Every weekend, year-round, hundreds of volunteers work on the trails and parks we love. They clear fallen branches, repair drainage, restore the natural habitat, and build new trails. Others volunteer as docents or citizen patrols to inform and aid other walkers. Without volunteers, our region's parks, wetlands, shoreline, and trails would not be what they are today.

Why volunteer? It's healthy, fun, and outdoorsy. It's companionable and educational, and it builds teamwork. It's great for the economy and helps the environment!

Learning about park and trail volunteer opportunities is as easy as visiting your city or county website, or asking at your favorite park office. There is so much that needs doing!

A GUIDE TO THIS BOOK

Walks in the core of the city are presented first (Southwest Portland, Northwest Portland and Forest Park, North Portland and Sauvie Island, Southeast Portland, and East Portland and Gresham), followed by the walks in the outer suburban areas (Vancouver, Southwest Washington, Columbia River Gorge, Clackamas County, and Washington County).

Walks within each chapter are arranged in approximate order of distance from downtown Portland. Each chapter begins with a locator map and a list of walks so you can easily choose where to go.

Each walk begins with a brief location description that places the walk very generally in reference to Portland's downtown area. Distances given are in driving miles (not as the crow flies) from an approximation of the city center.

Then follows a brief description line that includes the size of the park or trail area, the setting, and special attractions of the walk.

The address listed is the street location of the park or trailhead, not a mailing address. You may be able to use this for an Internet map search. If a park doesn't have a specific street address, we have provided a major cross street as a reference, following the common practice for most City of Portland parks.

A summary of the walk follows, with these headings:

TRAIL	Approximate length in miles.
STEEPNESS	Level (flat or nearly so), gentle (easy ups and downs), moderate (gets the heart rate up), or steep (stairs or equivalent steepness).
OTHER USES	Who shares the trail with you, the pedestrian. This might be bicycles or horses. Although they are not noted, expect to share paved trails with skaters. None of these walks allow motorized vehicles (with the exception of Lone Fir Cemetery).
DOGS	Three possibilities—on leash, off leash, or not allowed. (Designated off-leash areas may or may not include the trail.) Dog-friendly areas may be restricted.
CONNECTING TRAILS	Other trails (both included in this guide and not) that intersect the walk.
PARK AMENITIES	Restrooms (including freestanding facilities), interpretive walks, picnic tables, playgrounds, playing fields, et cetera. (Refer to maps and driving directions for parking information.)
DISABLED ACCESS	Americans with Disabilities Act (ADA) access, for the trail and/or park. (Call the listed office for details: their definition of "accessible" and yours may differ.) Some trails are barrier-free but don't meet ADA requirements.

A walk may have more than one setting, characterized by the following icons:

FOREST . . . .

RIVER/STREAM . . . .

LAKE/WETLAND . . . .

MEADOW/FARMLAND . . . .

NATURE PRESERVE . . . . .

MOUNTAIN VIEWS . . . .

BEACH . . . .

WATERFALL . . . .

CAMPSITE . . . .

Walk descriptions may include ecological, historical, and scenic information. They are not intended to be step-by-step trail guides; the goal is to entice and invite you to discover the pleasure of the walk on your own.

GETTING THERE: Driving directions in this book are basic and brief, from either downtown Portland or a major freeway; they will be of little help if you take a wrong turn. There may be public transport available to the trailhead or park. All parks listed are open daylight hours only unless otherwise noted.

CONTACT: Contact numbers may be for the individual park's office or a central parks department office. If there is an opportunity to volunteer at this park, it may be noted here.

MAPS: The map shown for each walk is intended to give a general sense of the layout of the park and trail. Do not rely on these to locate yourself in complex parks such as Forest Park, Lacamas Lake Regional Park, Hoyt Arboretum, and others with extensive trail systems. We have tried to show the major trails within each park, but there may be secondary paths that are not shown. Please follow guidelines and signs when walking as there may be problems with erosion and other hazards.

Map orientation is with north up, and the scale is approximate. The difference between paved, gravel, and natural surface trails is not indicated due to constantly changing conditions.

Map Legend

═══	ROAD	- -	TRAIL	
▬	DOCK/BOAT LAUNCH	Ⓟ	PARKING	
Ⓡ	RESTROOM	⋔	PICNIC AREA	
⌃	CAMPSITE	┼┼┼	RAILWAY	
▬·· ▬	PARK BOUNDARY	⊟	BRIDGE	
↟	FOREST	↓	WETLAND/MARSH	
⬬	WATER (RIVER, LAKE, POND)			

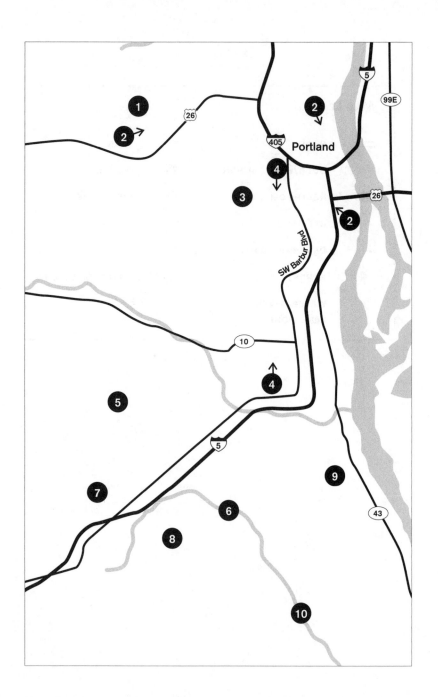

SOUTHWEST PORTLAND

1 HOYT ARBORETUM

Just west of downtown Portland

Discover a virtual tree museum on this hilly walk through a 187-acre arboretum in Washington Park.

TRAIL	Up to 12 miles
STEEPNESS	Moderate
OTHER USES	Pedestrians only
DOGS	On leash
CONNECTING TRAILS	Wildwood Trail, Marquam Trail (Walk #3)
PARK AMENITIES	Restrooms, staffed visitor center, interpretive displays, picnic shelters
DISABLED ACCESS	Overlook Trail, Bristlecone Pine Trail

Situated on 187 acres in Washington Park amid the Oregon Zoo, World Forestry Center, and Forest Park, this living tree museum began in 1931 as saplings on the site of a former county poor farm. The rolling terrain (and western Oregon's prodigious rains) were perfect for what has become a world-renowned tree fantasyland home to 6,000 individual trees, representing 2,300 unique species. Himalayan birch, Chilean monkey puzzles, snakebark maples, Brewer's weeping spruce (typically found only in the Siskiyou Mountains)—with so much to choose from and 12 miles of trail to explore it all, trying to find your favorite path (or the strangest tree) is like trying to decide on your favorite Portland microbrew. The choices are dizzying. You truly cannot go wrong. And even in the dead of winter, you'll find specimens like witch hazel flowering. But you can get lost. Picking up free trail maps that feature 30-minute, 1-hour, and 2-hour loops is a must.

Trees are divided by scientific classification and taxonomic arrangement, which, according to park history, was all the rage in the 1930s. SW Fairview Boulevard splits the park in the middle, separating the conifers on the west side from the deciduous trees on the east. Trail names such as Maple Trail, Oak Trail, and Beech Trail hint at what's in store. Trees are also neatly labeled with common and scientific names and their native ranges.

If it's sheer size you're after, follow the Redwood Trail, which begins just across

SW Fairview with a section of Japanese larches that sport pink cones in spring and yellow pine needles in fall, and Atlas cedars native to Morocco. Along this ravine-edge path you'll enter into a virtual woodland cathedral pillared with awe-inspiring coast redwoods and sequoias. An elevated deck at the end of the path juts into the canopy, creating an unforgettable tree-house chapel.

ADDRESS: 4000 SW Fairview Boulevard, Portland

GETTING THERE: From US 26 W, take exit 72 for the Oregon Zoo and turn right onto SW Canyon Road (which becomes SW Knights Boulevard). Go 0.8 mile, turn right on SW Fairview Boulevard, and look for the parking lot on the right. Metered parking is required from 9:30 a.m. to 5:00 p.m. There is MAX Light Rail access via the Washington Park stop.

CONTACT: Portland Parks and Recreation, (503) 865-8733, hoytarboretum.org

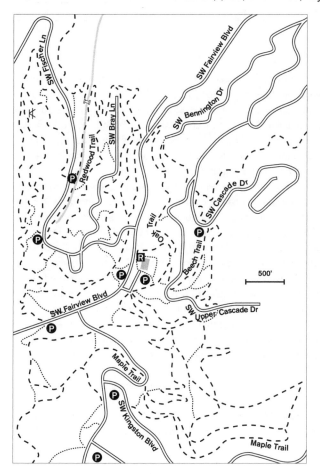

2 4T TRAIL

2.5 miles west of downtown Portland

Trails are just the start of this urban nature adventure that includes train, trolley, and tram rides.

TRAIL	4.5 miles
STEEPNESS	Moderate
OTHER USES	Pedestrians only
DOGS	On leash
CONNECTING TRAILS	Marquam Trail (Walk #3)
PARK AMENITIES	Picnic shelter, interpretive displays, viewpoints
DISABLED ACCESS	None

Named for the modes of travel you'll use to complete this outing—trail, tram, trolley, and train—the 4T could toss in another *T* for "terrific." Officially signposted in 2009, the trail portion follows a well-marked route on a network of nature paths in the West Hills and then links to Portland's abundance of public transit options. It adds up to an epic urban-meets-natural expedition. Complete the tour and you'll have visited Portland's highest point (and also its deepest) and floated above the city in one of the country's only aerial trams.

Walkers can embark from any point (Pioneer Courthouse Square, Washington Park, and the South Waterfront act as the 4T's main transit hubs) and head in either direction. But for a car-free route, start in Pioneer Courthouse Square, from which the MAX Light Rail (the train leg) delivers you to Washington Park via the Robertson Tunnel, the deepest subway tunnel in North America at 259 feet. Board the elevator to the surface, and follow the 4T signs downhill across the US 26 overpass.

Here the Marquam Trail, which is also signposted for the 4T, starts the first leg of the trail portion—a steepish, undulating climb to the top of Council Crest. Perched at 1,073 feet, this is Portland's tallest peak, delivering spectacular vistas of five Cascade volcanoes and a panorama of downtown. The second leg drops through Marquam Nature Park (Walk #3) on a 2-mile route that finishes with a steep walk to Oregon Health & Science University. Follow the 4T signs up to the upper terminal for the Portland Aerial Tram.

The bubble-shaped metallic cars beam riders 3,300 linear feet down to the South Waterfront in about 4 minutes—plenty of time to fill your iPhone with shots of Mount Hood, the Tilikum Crossing bridge, and the Willamette River. Heading downhill is free (the uphill fare is $4.55). But plan ahead: the tram runs Monday

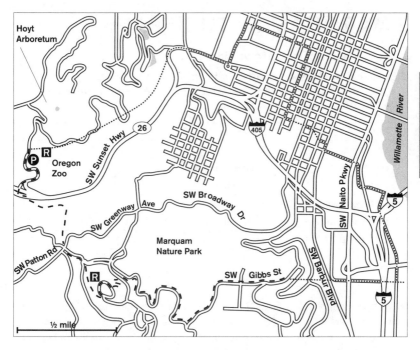

through Saturday year-round and Sunday afternoons from May to September. (Check the schedule and fares at gobytram.com.)

Down at the South Waterfront, complete the last leg of the 4T by taking the Portland Streetcar (the "trolley" part of the trail), which will deliver you just a few blocks west of Pioneer Courthouse Square.

ADDRESS: 4001 SW Canyon Road, Portland

GETTING THERE: All-day MAX Light Rail fare ($5) is required and is good for the Portland Streetcar as well. If driving to Washington Park, take US 26 W to exit 72 for the Oregon Zoo, and turn right onto SW Canyon Road. Park in the zoo lot. Metered parking is required.

CONTACT: MAX Light Rail, 503-238-7433, trimet.org; Portland Streetcar, 503-222-4200, portlandstreetcar.org; Portland Aerial Tram, 503-494-8283, gobytram.com

3 MARQUAM NATURE PARK

1.5 miles west of downtown Portland

Discover a level walking path in a thickly wooded 176-acre green space known for hilly terrain, ravines, big trees, and a connection to the lofty Council Crest Park.

TRAIL	1.6 miles
STEEPNESS	Moderate
OTHER USES	Pedestrians only
DOGS	On leash
CONNECTING TRAILS	4T Trail (Walk #2)
PARK AMENITIES	Picnic shelter, amphitheater, interpretive signs
DISABLED ACCESS	None

Aside from conjuring an image of a ravine with tall trees, cascading streams, and delicate flowers, Marquam Nature Park usually means one thing to walkers: hills. Set in a steep, forested draw on the slopes of Council Crest, Portland's highest point at 1,073 feet, the StairMaster-style terrain may feel imposing. But if you're willing to endure a short bout of legwork, you'll enjoy a wonderful near-level portion followed by an easy downhill walk back to the trailhead.

It's a wonder the park is here at all though. In the early twentieth century, the lower portion of Marquam Gulch had become one of the city's biggest garbage dumps. And in the late 1960s developers planned a large apartment complex in the ravine. Luckily greener heads prevailed. Today the park is a leafy jewel, with a lovely trailhead shelter filled with informative displays, handy trail maps, and tiled artwork. Multiple paths provide connections to Portland's 40-Mile Loop, Willamette Park, and Terwilliger Parkway (Walk #4), all thanks to dedicated steward-

ship by volunteers from Friends of Marquam Nature Park and other organizations.

Enjoy the fruits of their labor as you follow the Sunnyside Trail up a steep gravel path into the soaring firs. At 0.3 mile you'll come to an intersection with the Broadway Trail; keep left and cross a footbridge before a major junction for the 4T Trail (Walk #2), which rockets a mile up to Council Crest. But fear not, there's a relaxed option. Stay left, heading back into the ravine, via the Terwilliger Trail.

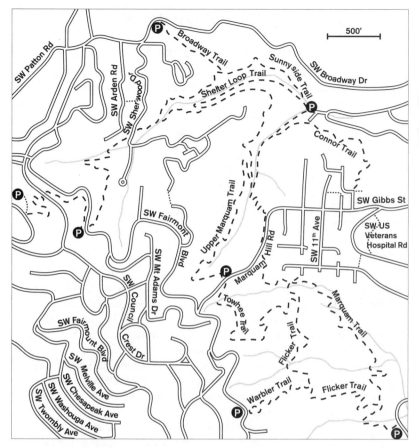

500'

The trail starts level and then dips down to a fence-lined switchback with sounds of a rushing creek rising up through the trees. At 0.7 mile, a trail junction heads back down to shelter, but stay straight for easy walking along a wonderfully level section with sweeping ravine views.

The trail continues into a wooded draw split by a stream. Across the footbridge, begin a small climb. Keep straight at the junction, turning down a short staircase and left (downhill) onto the Shelter Trail and back to the shelter.

ADDRESS: SW Marquam Street and Sam Jackson Park Road, Portland

GETTING THERE: From I-405 S, take exit 1C toward Ross Island Bridge and merge onto SW Broadway. Merge right onto SW 6th Avenue, following signs to Oregon Health & Science University. Continue on SW Sam Jackson Park Road and turn right onto SW Marquam Street to reach the park shelter and parking lot.

CONTACT: Portland Parks and Recreation, (503) 823-7529, portlandoregon.gov/parks

4 TERWILLIGER PARKWAY

1.5 miles southwest of downtown Portland

*Explore a 99-acre linear parkway winding through the West Hills,
linking natural areas, scenic overlooks, and a hidden history.*

TRAIL	3.2 miles round-trip as described here
STEEPNESS	Moderate
OTHER USES	Pedestrians only
DOGS	On leash
CONNECTING TRAILS	Marquam Trail (Walk #3)
PARK AMENITIES	Paved path, viewpoints, picnic tables
DISABLED ACCESS	Yes

Inspired by famed landscape architects the Olmsted brothers and their seminal 1903 Report of the Park Board, Terwilliger Parkway is a road in park's clothing. The drive's adjoining 3-mile pedestrian path, crouched in the woods below Oregon Health & Science University, enjoys massive firs and cedars, rows of cherry trees and rhododendrons, and sweeping Cascade vistas.

From the base of the parkway, Duniway Park Lilac Garden launders the air with the aroma of more than 125 varieties of lilacs. Climb to the left to take in views of the eastside buttes and the Tillikum Crossing bridge, and pass beneath the silver bubble of the Portland Aerial Tram.

At 0.9 mile, a set of hidden staircases appear. Rising 145 steps into the trees, they lead to the VA Portland Health Care System hospital and are a popular feature for runners. Now for quirky scavenger-hunt fun, try to spy the

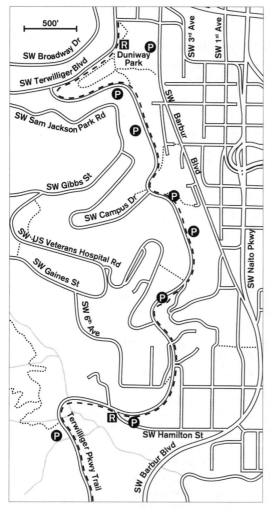

mossed-over relics of the Portland Health Course. Opened in 1974, it's a circuit of old-school workout stations (think metal rings, chin-up bars, and an only-in-Portland log-twisting apparatus) that are now being swallowed by the forest along the path.

Just beyond the VA hospital, a more recent feature awaits. In 2014 the city acquired an acre off SW Lowell Lane from private hands to establish Eagle Point, a viewpoint with jaw-dropping Mount Hood sight lines. It's one of two such vantage points the Olmsted brothers originally envisioned for the road.

At 1.6 miles arrive at the second lookout: Elk Point, tucked next to the Chart House restaurant. A large totem pole guards the overlook of the Willamette River and the mountains beyond. For most, this marks a scenic turnaround, but the path continues about 0.5 mile to SW Barbur Boulevard.

ADDRESS: SW 6th Avenue and Sheridan Street, Portland

GETTING THERE: From US 26 W, take exit 1C and follow SW Broadway and then SW 6th approximately 0.4 mile to Terwilliger Parkway. Parking is available along Terwilliger but is limited.

CONTACT: Portland Parks and Recreation, (503) 823-7529, portlandoregon.gov/parks

5 GABRIEL PARK

7 miles southwest of downtown Portland

Walk broad park lawns, then disappear into a hidden forested ravine in this classic 90-acre city park.

TRAIL	Up to 3 miles
STEEPNESS	Gentle to moderate
OTHER USES	Pedestrians only
DOGS	On leash; off-leash area
CONNECTING TRAILS	None
PARK AMENITIES	Restrooms, sports fields, dog park, skate park, tennis and volleyball courts
DISABLED ACCESS	Yes

Gabriel Park should come with a warning label: "May cause park envy."

At 90 acres, this Southwest Portland gem offers up just about everything you could ask for in a local green space. Tucked among the broad, hilly lawns, there are baseball fields, tennis courts, community gardens, a honey of a skate park, and very popular seasonal off-leash dog areas.

Yet if you just want to get away, you can do that too. Along the southern portions of the park, a screen of western red cedars, hemlocks, and firs rise like a cliff and shade a pair of creeks and a deep ravine. Approximately 3 miles of paths wind around all the park's facets, offering gentle paved routes along with counterpoint dirt-track adventures. A central paved path runs the width of the park, about 0.5 mile, between SW 45th Avenue and SW 37th Avenue; the wilder parts of the trail are south of this path.

For a good introduction to the woodsy corridors of the park, start from the tennis courts along SW 45th Avenue and head south, following the paved path directly

between the two smaller courts, with the summer off-leash dog area to the right. Ahead you'll pass a restored wetland meadow area with pretty pink hardhack flowers and fluttering visitors like tiger swallowtail butterflies and Anna's hummingbirds.

A little wooden bridge over Vermont Creek marks the entrance to the ravine. From here you can continue up a short distance to reach a hallway-like meadow traversed by a paved path between tall stands of trees and then drop back into the woods near the baseball diamond. To explore the large central ravine, use the creek as a guide, and walk along the wooden fence beneath the wide umbrella of tall western red cedars.

At approximately 0.4 mile you'll exit the forest and meet the central paved path. Long daisy-dotted meadows line the path back to the trailhead and invite sunny-day frolicking.

ADDRESS: SW Vermont and SW 45th Avenue, Portland

GETTING THERE: From I-5 S, take exit 269B for Multnomah Boulevard. Continue 0.7 mile and turn right on SW 35th Avenue. Go 0.6 mile and turn left on SW Vermont Street. Then go 0.5 mile and turn left on SW 45th Avenue. Look for the park entrance on the left.

CONTACT: Portland Parks and Recreation, (503) 823-7529, portlandoregon.gov/parks

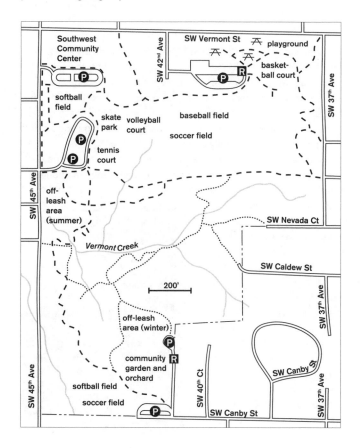

<u>6</u> MARSHALL PARK

7 miles south of downtown Portland

Discover Tryon Creek's other natural area hidden inside a 26-acre canyon in Southwest Portland.

TRAIL	Approximately 2 miles
STEEPNESS	Moderate
OTHER USES	Pedestrians only
DOGS	On leash
CONNECTING TRAILS	None
PARK AMENITIES	Play structure, interpretive display, picnic area
DISABLED ACCESS	None

Before it flows through its namesake park, Tryon Creek has a warm-up act—and it's a good one. As the centerpiece of 26-acre Marshall Park, just northwest of Tryon Creek State Natural Area (Walk #10), the stream tumbles through the middle of a 400-foot-wide canyon, echoing off towers of sea-green Douglas firs and western red cedars as it washes over flat slabs of black rocks. At the base of the glen, a newly installed playground and natural play area filled with logs and smooth stones make this an ideal day trip for family outings.

From the SW 18th Place trailhead on the park's western sidewall, you can drop either left or right about 0.3 mile to the center of the park, where a circular gravel path surrounds the play area. Near a large interpretive sign detailing the creek's various macroinvertebrates (caddisflies and crayfish, among others), a small stone-arch footbridge crosses Tryon Creek beneath a grotto-like cliff face.

A few paces beyond the stone bridge, a spur trail tracks left, following Tryon Creek's southerly flow about 0.2 mile along a ridgeline to a road crossing at SW 12th Place. From there, the path drops around 0.3 mile to meet the stream at a large log crossing. You can follow the flow to SW Boones Ferry Road and reach Tryon Creek State Natural Area, but the track is muddy and faint.

After a few balance beam attempts on the log, double back to the stone bridge and

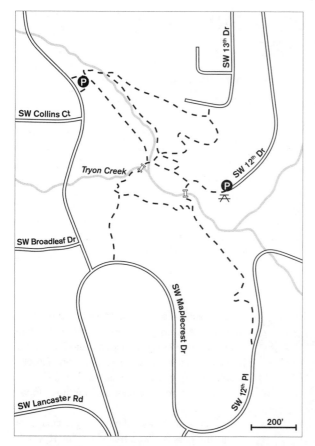

head uphill on a zigzagging fence post–lined trail that wraps back down to the creek at a wooden bridge near the playground. Below the bridge the creek forms a dark pool fed by tiny cascades. Cross the bridge and head left, then follow a small set of wooden stairs to the right to a wide path rising gently above the ravine back to the trailhead.

ADDRESS: SW 18th Place and SW Collins Court, Portland

GETTING THERE: From I-5 S, take exit 296A for SW Barbur Boulevard, go right, and quickly turn right again on SW Spring Garden Street. Go 0.3 mile and turn right on SW 17th Avenue. Then go 0.3 mile, turn right on SW Taylors Ferry Road, and turn left on SW 18th Place. Look for the park on the left, before SW Collins Court.

CONTACT: Portland Parks and Recreation, (503) 823-7529, portlandoregon.gov/parks

7 WOODS MEMORIAL NATURAL AREA

5 miles southwest of downtown Portland

A 36-acre gem hides just out of sight and offers a quick, woodsy escape.

TRAIL	1.5 miles
STEEPNESS	Gentle to moderate
OTHER USES	Pedestrians only
DOGS	On leash
CONNECTING TRAILS	None
PARK AMENITIES	None
DISABLED ACCESS	0.5 mile of SW Wood Parkway

The 36-acre Woods Memorial Natural Area occupies a deep glen filled with a blend of big-leaf maples, western hemlocks, and firs. At the base of the ravine, two forks of Woods Creek dribble down, feeding the larger Fanno Creek Watershed through a filter of smoothed stones and fallen logs.

Once a mishmash of muddy, unofficial user trails, the park is now a beneficiary of 15 years of hands-on love from volunteer groups like Friends of Woods Park and SW Trails. Paths are well marked (signs mirror the familiar retro vibe of Forest Park's waymarks). Three small bridges—Low Bridge, Middle Bridge, and High Bridge—crisscross the creek, having replaced haphazardly strewn branches and boards, allowing stable links to either side of the park.

Begin on the paved SW Wood Parkway. Closed to cars, this curving 0.5-mile road forms the western boundary, with natural trails linked to its northern and southern ends. Along a small meadow being restored to boost pollinator habitat, the aptly named Stairway Trail descends box-like steps 200 feet to the creek. Cross Low Bridge to explore the short Cedar Trail to the left, where you'll find a cluster of western red cedars. On the right, Woods Creek Trail heads up on a series of boardwalks leading to Middle Bridge and High Bridge. Wherever sun pierces the leaves, spiky common horsetail and buttercups bloom profusely. Low in the glen, birds remain mostly out of sight. But songs are ever present. The call of the black-capped chickadee is likely to echo throughout the ravine.

Above High Bridge, Woods Creek Trail goes up a set of pretty stairs leading to neighborhood trailheads. To make a nice loop, cross over High Bridge and follow the creek up South Trail until you come to the southern end of SW Wood Parkway. Turn right to return to the start, keeping an eye out for a few cherry trees and horse chestnut trees shading the way.

ADDRESS: SW 45th Drive and SW Wood Parkway, Portland

GETTING THERE: From SW Barbur Boulevard, head south and turn right on SW Taylors Ferry Road. Go 0.2 mile (crossing over SW Capitol Highway) and turn right at SW 48th Avenue, which becomes SW 45th Drive. Go 0.1 mile and look for the park sign and entrance on the right. Park along SW Wood Parkway.

CONTACT: Portland Parks and Recreation, (503) 823-7529, portlandoregon.gov/parks

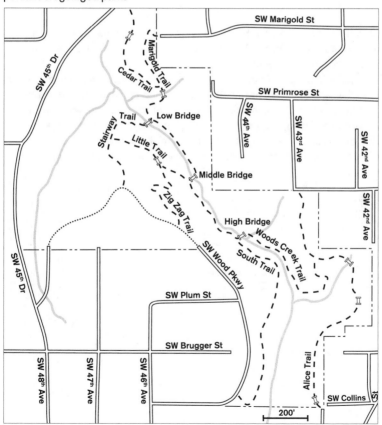

8 MARICARA NATURAL AREA

8 miles southwest of downtown Portland

This kid-friendly hike is bound to leave children enchanted with the natural world.

TRAIL	Approximately 1 mile
STEEPNESS	Gentle
OTHER USES	Pedestrians only
DOGS	On leash
CONNECTING TRAILS	SW Trails 5
PARK AMENITIES	None
DISABLED ACCESS	None

This pocket-size natural area in Southwest Portland surely ranks as the city's most enchanting natural area. Why? A resident population of forest fairies—or at least their tree houses—can be found here.

Throughout Maricara's 17 acres, which stretch across a gentle, wooded slope in the tree-blessed Markham neighborhood, you'll find trunks of firs and maples that have been whimsically adorned with tiny hand-painted doors, windows, and mirrors, all move-in ready for a family of pixies. It's a playful game of hide-and-seek around the park's easy loop trail to find them all. (Some rest in tree hollows. Some are high up in the branches. One even has an apartment number.) The fairy

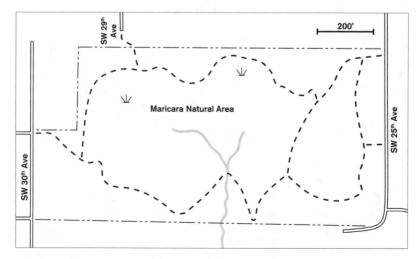

houses are a good indicator that this park is a frequent destination of Ladybug Nature Walks, a popular naturalist program for kids run by the Portland Parks and Recreation Department.

There's plenty of real-deal nature journaling for kids (or adults) to do here as well. Start with the fact that dribbling Arnold Creek drains into Tryon Creek State Natural Area (Walk #10) just to the west and helps feed a small wetland area. Or try cataloging numerous kinds of ferns, including sword, licorice, and lady. For sketching, there are Indian plums and Oregon grapes. Woodland wildflowers like Columbia lilies could trigger discussions of pollination. Extra points for sighting a resident northern flicker pecking on a snag.

Recent trail work includes more than 0.25 miles of new trail and 0.5 mile of repaired paths, so the walking has never been better. For those in need of more distance, exit the park's eastern edge on SW 25th Street, and follow the brown signs marking SW Trails 5, which zigzags along low-traffic streets and splotches of greenery for 1.5 miles until it reaches the northern tip of Tryon Creek State Natural Area.

ADDRESS: 10608 SW 30th Avenue, Portland

GETTING THERE: From I-5 S, take exit 295 for Capitol Highway and turn right on SW Taylors Ferry Road, then right again on SW Capitol Highway and left on SW Huber Street. Go 0.3 mile and turn right on SW 35th Avenue, then left on SW Maricara Street. Look for the trailhead at the end of the road, at the intersection with SW 30th Avenue. Park along SW 30th Avenue.

CONTACT: Portland Parks and Recreation, (503) 823-7529, portlandoregon.gov/parks

9 RIVER VIEW NATURAL AREA

7 miles south of downtown Portland

Find lightly trodden paths in this out-of-the-way 146-acre city park.

TRAIL	Up to 2.5 miles
STEEPNESS	Moderate to steep
OTHER USES	Mountain bicycles
DOGS	On leash
CONNECTING TRAILS	None
PARK AMENITIES	None
DISABLED ACCESS	None

It's a solid bet: visit this 146-acre natural area on even the sunniest of days, and you'll scarcely encounter another soul.

Abutting Lewis & Clark College deep in Southwest Portland, and just a stone's throw from Tryon Creek State Natural Area, River View boasts all the attributes of a premier destination. Among the heavy tree cover rich with alders, vine maples, and western red cedars, seven streams dance down the hillsides, dropping fresh cold water to the Willamette River. More than seventy bird species have been recorded here, along with thirty different kinds of mammals. So why aren't more people drawn in?

Lack of awareness is a factor. River View was acquired by Portland Parks and Recreation (in partnership with Metro) in 2011. Entrances are still informal. There's minimal signage, and there are no officially mapped trails. Controversy is another factor: in 2015, city officials somewhat infamously banned mountain bikers from the trails, even though bikers had ridden here for years with the knowledge of the former land owner, River View Cemetery. Protests ensued. The city says more studies on the issue are pending.

Regardless of the cyclist hullabaloo, River View remains a joy for bipedal movement. Though keep in mind that, as management plans are being formalized, trails are unofficial. And plenty of restoration work is afoot. (Up to fifty thousand plants and shrubs have been planted, and loads of invasive ivy have been culled.)

The best entrance is from the top of the park, along SW Palatine Hill Road. Along this forested lip, think of the park like a ski area: trails funnel down to a mostly level path that parallels SW Macadam Avenue, which bounds the eastern park edge below. Lewis & Clark College borders the southern perimeter, to the right. In between, a few cutoffs split the middle, folding into gorgeous ravines. One subtle feature to observe is a number of nurse logs and stumps (evidence that the park was logged as recently as the 1950s) slowly decomposing into a second-growth forest, along with large snags—virtual flypaper for the hairy woodpecker, one of River View's noisier residents.

ADDRESS: SW Palatine Hill Road and SW Brugger Street, Portland

GETTING THERE: From I-5 S, exit Terwilliger Boulevard. Go 1.5 miles to a round-about, bear right onto SW Palater Road (following signs for Lewis & Clark College), and quickly turn left onto SW Palatine Hill Road. Go 0.1 mile, turn left onto SW Brugger Street, and park along the road. Find the trailhead at the intersection of SW Brugger Street and SW Palatine Hill Road.

CONTACT: Portland Parks and Recreation, (503) 823-7529, portlandoregon.gov/parks

<u>10</u> TRYON CREEK STATE NATURAL AREA

Portland, 7 miles south of downtown

Oregon's only state park located in a major city delivers a 658-acre natural escape.

TRAIL	8 miles total; 2-mile loop as described here
STEEPNESS	Gentle, with one steep section
OTHER USES	Horses
DOGS	On leash
CONNECTING TRAILS	None
PARK AMENITIES	Nature center, restrooms, trail maps, interpretive programs
DISABLED ACCESS	Trillium Trail

Tryon Creek State Natural Area reigns as Southwest Portland's most visited forested attraction. And not just for walkers. An annual trillium festival, summer concerts, and nature camps make this 658-acre park as much a community hub as a hiking destination.

Up to 8 miles of trails spill down into the canyon from the staffed nature center, where you'll find trail maps, displays, and insight from park rangers. For a quick introduction, start on the wonderful ADA-compliant loop trail beside the nature center. This 0.3-mile path includes a pair of overlooks and displays about forest residents. The presence of North American flying squirrels, a nocturnal species, will likely grab your attention. (And since trails stay open till 9:00 p.m., you might see one midflight.)

The Old Main Trail, a mostly paved, wide path constructed by the Civilian Conservation Corps in 1930s, is the park's most popular trail, dropping down 100 feet to the lush ravine core and namesake creek. The creek sees

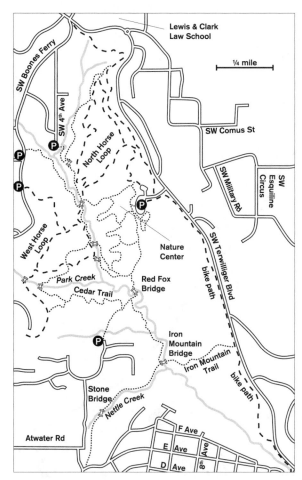

Lewis & Clark
Law School

¼ mile

SW Comus St

SW Boones Ferry

SW 4th Ave

North Horse Loop

SW Military Rd

SW Esquiline Circus

SW Terwilliger Blvd
bike path

West Horse Loop

Nature
Center

Park Creek

Cedar Trail

Red Fox
Bridge

Iron
Mountain
Bridge

Iron Mountain Trail

bike path

Stone
Bridge

Nettle Creek

F Ave

E Ave

D Ave

8th Ave

Atwater Rd

drastic seasonal fluctuations yet still provides a reliable habitat for trout. From the creek, cross Obie's Bridge and follow the creek northward, turning right on the West Horse Loop to meet the Middle Creek Trail.

Just past 0.5 mile, start a slow climb above the creek near a wetland restoration area. Follow a small boardwalk to a set of rustic wood steps and then keep right to cross High Bridge. A major junction lies ahead, with the Middle Creek Trail leading back to the trailhead. Here take a 0.25-mile detour up Lewis and Clark Trail (the college abuts the northern tip of the park) to find the Terry Riley Bridge, a joyously wobbly wood-planked miniature suspension bridge tucked away in a gulch. Listen for one of the park's five species of woodpeckers, and watch birds like cedar waxwings and dark-eyed juncos fluttering through a small break in the canopy.

Back on the Middle Creek Trail, head briefly up a steep ridgeline. Then follow signs for the Maple Ridge and Center Trails, which wind gently among large maples and alders to the nature center.

ADDRESS: 11321 SW Terwilliger Boulevard, Portland

GETTING THERE: From I-5 S, take exit 297 for Barbur Boulevard, and quickly turn right onto Terwilliger Boulevard. Go approximately 2 miles (bearing right through a roundabout), and look for the park entrance on the right.

CONTACT: Oregon State Parks, (503) 636-9886, oregonstateparks.org

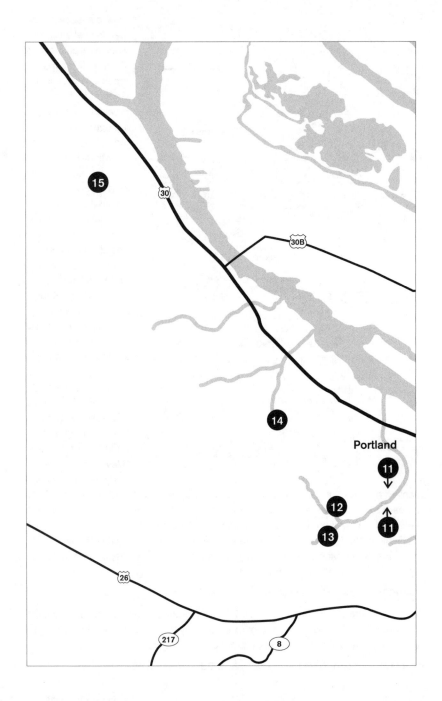

NORTHWEST PORTLAND & FOREST PARK

<u>11</u> LOWER MACLEAY PARK TO PITTOCK MANSION

2.5 miles northwest of downtown Portland

Take a heart-pumping walk from a deep forest canyon to a city panorama by Pittock Mansion.

TRAIL	2.5 miles one way; 5 miles round-trip
STEEPNESS	Gentle to steep
OTHER USES	Pedestrians only
DOGS	On leash
CONNECTING TRAILS	Wildwood Trail, Pittock Bird Sanctuary (Walk #12), Collins and Uhtoff Sanctuaries (Walk #13)
PARK AMENITIES	Restrooms at Lower Macleay Park and Pittock Mansion, interpretive displays
DISABLED ACCESS	Lower Macleay Trail's first 0.25 mile

If Portland had an official power walk, this would be it. Rising 800 feet in 2.5 miles, the trail leads from Forest Park's tree-filled Balch Creek Canyon to Pittock Mansion, the stunning former residence of Portland's original newspaper tycoon, Henry Pittock. If the verticality gives you pause, fear not. Walkers of all stripes routinely brave the route, and the sights along the way provide loads of incentive.

Starting in Macleay Park, beneath the Thurman Street Bridge, the Lower Macleay Trail provides a dramatic prologue to the wonders of Forest Park. Designated as a National Recreation Trail, the nearly mile-long path lines Balch Creek, the park's largest stream, replete with meandering bends and miniature cascades. The clear creek waters support an isolated population of cutthroat trout. On either side, the chasm walls are hung with ferns and sky-poking trees.

Just short of 1 mile, keep a sharp eye on the left side of the trail for a plaque noting the tallest Douglas fir in the city. Last measured in 1997, the behemoth measures 242 feet (though it's likely grown even taller) and may be 450 years old. The Stone House, a classic Portland oddity, is 100 yards ahead. A relic from the Works Progress Administration (WPA) era, it served as a park restroom until it was ravaged by the legendary Columbus Day storm of 1962. The delightfully spooky remains earned the alternate nickname the Witch's Castle and have even appeared in the Portland-based television show *Grimm*.

Continue along the creek on the Wildwood Trail to a switchbacking ascent to Upper Macleay Park and the Audubon Society of Portland headquarters. Across NW Cornell Road, the Wildwood Trail begins a swooping 0.5-mile climb through

a grand assemblage of hillside firs, offering occasional glances of the canyon below.

The trail exits into the parking area for Pittock Mansion. Drop down to the garden-lined lawns of this opulent abode. Built in 1914, the twenty-two-room French Renaissance–style landmark is a marvel even by today's standards. (Pittock installed the latest technologies of the day, like an elevator, a refrigerator room, and thermostat-controlled heating.) Daily tours and a museum store offer more insight. Plan to spend extra time just admiring the view. On clear days you can survey Portland's skyline dwarfed by five Cascade volcanoes.

ADDRESS: 2960 NW Upshur Street, Portland

GETTING THERE: From I-405 N, take exit 3 for US 30, then exit on NW Vaughn Street. Turn left onto NW 23rd Avenue. Turn right onto NW Thurman Street. Turn right onto NW 28th Avenue, then take a quick left onto NW Upshur Street, and continue to Macleay Park.

CONTACT: Portland Parks and Recreation, (503) 823-7529, portlandoregon.gov/parks

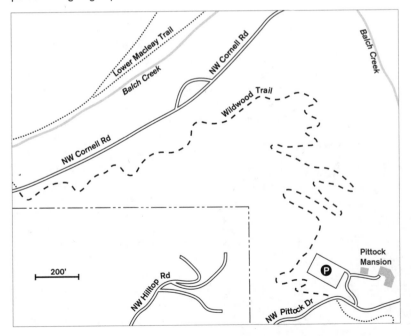

12 AUDUBON SOCIETY OF PORTLAND PITTOCK BIRD SANCTUARY

3 miles northwest of downtown Portland

The Audubon Society of Portland headquarters provides a home base for a woodsy, family-friendly adventure.

TRAIL	Approximately 1.3 miles
STEEPNESS	Gentle to moderate
OTHER USES	Pedestrians only
DOGS	Not allowed
CONNECTING TRAILS	Collins and Uhtoff Sanctuaries (Walk #13), Wildwood Trail
PARK AMENITIES	Audubon Society of Portland headquarters: Nature Store, interpretive center, maps, guided walks, Wildlife Care Center, restrooms
DISABLED ACCESS	None

Nestled in a ravine amid Forest Park's expansive tree-stacked ripples, the Audubon Society of Portland's Pittock Bird Sanctuary consists of 30 acres of the group's larger 150-acre reserve along NW Cornell Road. Set within minutes of downtown, it's an ideal destination for kids or for anyone with kid-like curiosity.

Here you'll find the society's local headquarters, home to a visitor center brimming with a nature bookstore, a gift shop, and interpretive exhibits. A short, easy

trail system drops down from the visitor center, accessing pockets of remnant old-growth Douglas firs estimated at 250 to 300 years old and measuring up to 255 feet tall. Balch Creek trickles through a lush gulch leading past Forest Park's only pond, where you might find Pacific giant salamanders and rough-skinned newts lounging.

The engaging setting comes with its own set of personal greeters in the form of Audubon's education birds. These injured or mistreated birds that can no longer live in the wild now act as forest ambassadors and live in a series of large enclosures near the trailhead. They include Ruby the turkey vulture, Jack the American kestrel, and Aristophanes, a large common raven that can imitate human speech. A series of windows also lets you peek into the Audubon Society's Wildlife Care Center, where injured birds are treated.

Once down the slope, the bird chatter continues amid a thick shroud of trees. Cross gurgling Balch Creek on a pretty bridge and you'll reach the gazebo-lined pond. From there you can wind up the Jay Trail, which wraps around a grove of ancient cedars and firs. One especially massive fir comes with a bench-lined platform wrapped around it, providing the ultimate forest rest stop.

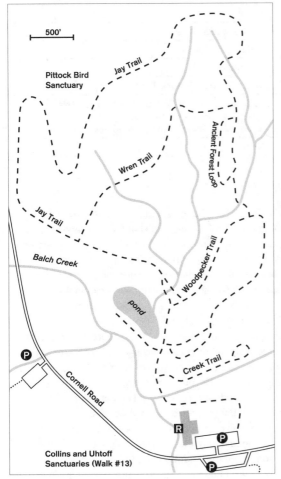

ADDRESS: 5151 NW Cornell Road, Portland

GETTING THERE: From I-5 N, take the Fremont Bridge exit, cross the bridge, and exit onto Vaughn Street. Go to NW 25th Avenue and turn left. Continue to NW Lovejoy Street and turn right. NW Lovejoy becomes NW Cornell Road. Continue 1.5 miles (through two tunnels) and look for the nature store on the right. Additional parking is available across the street.

CONTACT: Audubon Society of Portland, (503) 292-6855, audubon portland.org

13 AUDUBON SOCIETY OF PORTLAND COLLINS AND UHTOFF SANCTUARIES

3.3 miles northwest of downtown Portland

A pair of interconnected Audubon Society nature reserves provide a lesser-traveled path with deep ravines, large trees, and Forest Park's largest woodpecker.

TRAIL	1.3-mile loop
STEEPNESS	Gentle to moderate
OTHER USES	Pedestrians only
DOGS	Not allowed
CONNECTING TRAILS	Wildwood Trail, Pittock Bird Sanctuary (Walk #12)
PARK AMENITIES	Audubon Society of Portland headquarters: Nature Store, interpretive center, maps, guided walks, Wildlife Care Center, restrooms
DISABLED ACCESS	None

While the Audubon Society's Pittock Bird Sanctuary just across the road sees heavy use, the trails of the interconnected Collins and Uhtoff Sanctuaries feel like your own private reserve by comparison. The first parcels here were snapped up by the Audubon Society in 1982 and have grown to 120 acres. Logged in the 1800s and then again in the 1950s, the forests here still contain scatterings of large hemlocks, Douglas firs, and maples and have bounced back thanks to intensive and ongoing restoration efforts by both Metro and Audubon Society volunteers. An easy loop walk will take you through both of the reserves.

Treks begin directly across NW Cornell Road from the Audubon Society, where Founders Trail rises up into a red alder forest, passing a nursery. A series of labeled flora is representative of the terrain you'll be exploring: big-leaf maples and native blackberry, salmonberry, and Indian plum. Several hefty snags here have been vigorously drilled by resident pileated woodpeckers, and sightings of this species of woodpecker are so frequent that the path's been dubbed Woodpecker Trail.

After dipping in and out of a series of ravines, Founders Trail meets an intersection with South Collins Trail. Heading right drops you straight down to the Collins Trailhead, just up the road from the Audubon headquarters. Stick left to complete the loop, which rises slowly into more red alder and maples, making it a particularly good spot to expect autumn colors.

Ahead pass through two fern-loaded hillsides and join North Collins Trail, which continues down a gorgeous cascading boardwalk. The canopy eventually opens, and the hillsides and ridges soak in sun, allowing for good wildflower showings. The trail leads back down the hill and over a pair of bridges to the Collins Trailhead, about 100 yards up from the Pittock Sanctuary.

ADDRESS: 5151 NW Cornell Road, Portland

GETTING THERE: From I-5 N, take the Fremont Bridge exit, cross the bridge, and exit at Vaughn Street. Go to NW 25th Avenue and turn left. Continue to NW Lovejoy Street and turn right. NW Lovejoy becomes NW Cornell Road. Continue 1.5 miles (through two tunnels) and look for the nature center on the right. Parking is available across the street.

CONTACT: Audubon Society of Portland, (503) 292-6855, audubonportland.org

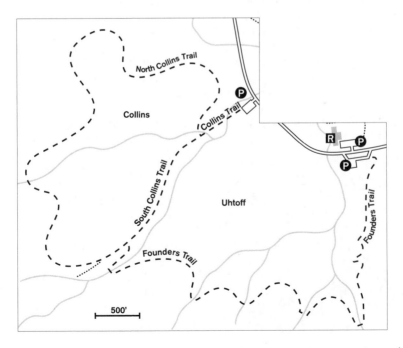

14 FOREST PARK NATURE TRAIL LOOP–FROM FIRELANE 1

5 miles northwest of downtown Portland

Explore a quiet section of central Forest Park.

TRAIL	3-mile loop
STEEPNESS	Moderate
OTHER USES	Bicycles on Firelane 1 and Leif Erikson Drive
DOGS	On leash
CONNECTING TRAILS	Chestnut Trail, Firelane 1, Leif Erikson Drive, Morak Trail, Wildwood Trail
PARK AMENITIES	None
DISABLED ACCESS	None

If you like quiet ravines, sun-soaked ridgelines, trickling creeks, and an out-of-the-way feel, then consider this your backdoor entrance into Forest Park, with access to all-star tracks like Wildwood Trail and Leif Erikson Drive that are well away from popular entry points Macleay Park and NW Thurman Street.

Starting from a hidden trailhead on NW Forest Lane, Firelane 1 undulates on a wide track filled with Columbia lilies, red columbine, and fluttering red admiral butterflies. Keep straight past junctions with Morak Trail and Wildwood Trail, and the path will drop to a small grassy patch with an inviting picnic table. Just to the left, the Nature Trail begins a nearly mile-long zigzag among towering maple, fir, and western hemlock trees, Oregon grape, and forking creeks.

At 0.8 mile ignore a tie-in with Wildwood Trail, and follow Nature Trail into the south fork of Rocking Chair Creek, which is said to be named for a rocking chair

found here many years ago. (Spotting recently hatched blue robin eggs or osprey feathers is more likely today.) As the trail lowers, the ravine closes in, and you'll brush against ferns and trickling little falls. Just beyond a gate at the 1.1-mile mark, Nature Trail ends and you'll connect with Leif Erikson Drive.

To the left follow Chestnut Trail up the north fork of Rocking

Chair Creek. Exposed sections of basalt rock border this tucked-away trail. At 1.7 miles turn left on Wildwood Trail (a metal trail map marks the junction), then skip a link to Nature Trail and stay on Wildwood Trail, which wraps back through a grand avenue of giant Douglas firs on a track above Nature Trail. By 2.6 miles you'll loop back to Firelane 1. Head right to return to the trailhead.

ADDRESS: NW Forest Lane and NW 53rd Drive, Portland

GETTING THERE: On NW Cornell Road drive 0.8 mile past the Audubon Society Sanctuary, and turn right on NW Thompson Road. Drive 0.9 mile and turn right on NW 53rd Avenue, then make a quick left on Forest Lane / Firelane 1. Continue straight to the trailhead.

CONTACT: Portland Parks and Recreation, (503) 823-7529, portlandoregon.gov/parks

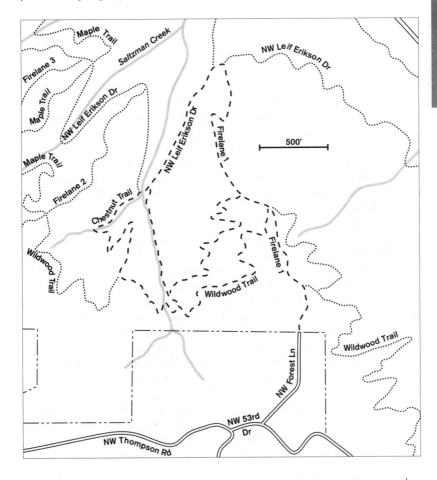

15 FOREST PARK FIRELANE 15 LOOP

12 miles northwest of downtown Portland

Discover 4 miles of Forest Park's scenic, little-traveled northern trails.

TRAIL	4.2 miles
STEEPNESS	Moderate to steep
OTHER USES	Bicycles on Firelane 15, Firelane 12, BPA Road
DOGS	On leash
CONNECTING TRAILS	Firelane 12, BPA Road, Wildwood Trail
PARK AMENITIES	None
DISABLED ACCESS	None

Situated at the far northern edge of Forest Park, where park boundaries blend into the larger Coast Range ecosystems, this approximately 4-mile loop is rife with inspiring vistas, wildflowers, and gargantuan trees.

Along Firelane 15, you'll dip and climb along a power-line corridor—a prime location to view wildlife such as coyotes, black-tailed deer, and elk—rising to one of the park's finest panoramas: a nearly 360-degree survey of Mounts Saint Helens and Adams, Sauvie Island, lonely barges on the Willamette River, and the blue-tinted Coast Range.

Follow Firelane 15 into the woods to find secretive Kielhorn Meadow. Unique in the park (aerial analysis shows that the park is 99 percent forest), this tree-encircled open space begs for picnicking or simply pausing to listen for warblers, robins, or perhaps northern pygmy owls, which are active during the day. Back on Firelane 15, the path veers down nearly a mile and settles into a shadow-enveloped ravine cradling Miller Creek, one of the park's few trout-supporting streams.

Next ascend Firelane 12 (a lung-taxing endeavor) to meet BPA Road, a power-line corridor maintained by the Bonneville Power Administration (BPA). Large red-tailed hawks and bald eagles routinely flock here, searching the open space for voles and other tasty treats. The sunny exposure means eye-catching wildflower displays. Look for Oregon iris, orange honeysuckle, and western columbine, to name just a few.

Along this junction, a small bronze plaque fixed on a grouping of stones pays tribute to a significant grassroots effort that saved the surrounding 73 acres—which became known as the "Hole in the Park"—from development in the 1990s. For one last treat, turn right on the famed Wildwood Trail, where a 0.5-mile section boasts everything that makes this trail such a joy to walk. With nearly level grading and blue diamond trail markings painted on trees ticking off 0.25-mile sections, the trail zips over a string of footbridges to meet back with Firelane 15 for the walk out.

ADDRESS: NW Skyline Drive between NW Germantown Road and NW Newberry Road, Portland

GETTING THERE: From I-405 N, take US 30 W, drive 4 miles (passing the Saint Johns Bridge), and turn left onto NW Germantown Road. At NW Skyline Boulevard turn right, go 1.4 miles, and look for a small pullout on the right, marked by a green gate and a sign for Firelane 15.

CONTACT: Portland Parks and Recreation, (503) 823-7529, portlandoregon.gov/parks

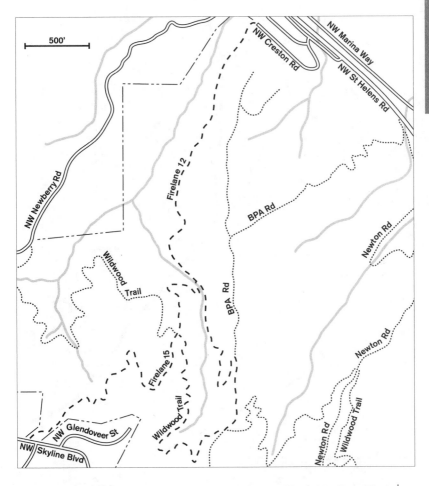

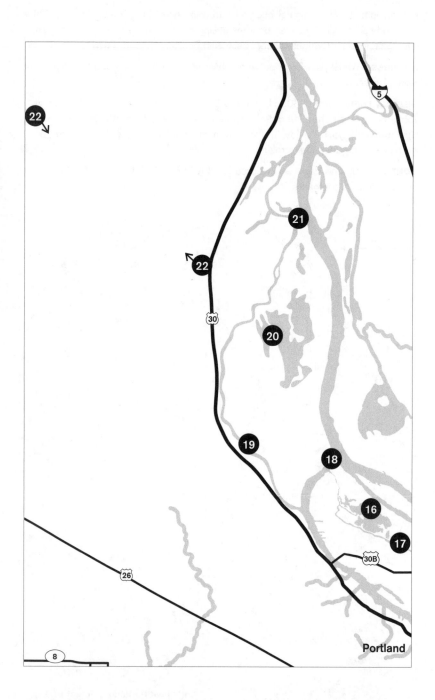

NORTH PORTLAND & SAUVIE ISLAND

<u>16</u> SMITH AND BYBEE WETLANDS NATURAL AREA

9.5 miles north of downtown Portland

A flat paved trail accesses a pair of bird blinds overlooking the country's largest urban wetland.

TRAIL	Approximately 1 mile
STEEPNESS	Gentle
OTHER USES	Pedestrians only
DOGS	Not allowed
CONNECTING TRAILS	40-Mile Loop
PARK AMENITIES	Restrooms, interpretive displays, canoe/kayak launch
DISABLED ACCESS	Yes

Arguably Portland's best paddling destination, Smith and Bybee Wetlands Natural Area (a.k.a. Smith and Bybee Lakes) is the largest urban wetland area in the country, with 2,000 acres in the Portland city limits. The waters hold what may be the state's biggest population of western painted turtles. Beavers and river otters, along with deer and coyotes on the forest fringes, are frequently seen. And if it flies, you'll probably find it here, including summer residents like white pelicans.

While paddlers will probably get the lion's share of sightings, the window for boat travel is short: from April to July, before lake waters recede. But walkers are in luck year-round, thanks to the paved ADA-compliant Interlakes Trail, which bisects the lakes, offering a quick out-and-back walk. Not that you'll want to rush it.

Accessed from the trailhead after a 0.2-mile walk on the paved 40-Mile Loop path, the Interlakes Trail turns off into the woods, burrowing between a tunnel of black cottonwood, pacific willow, Oregon ash, and snowberry. Within the first 0.5 mile, you'll pass a

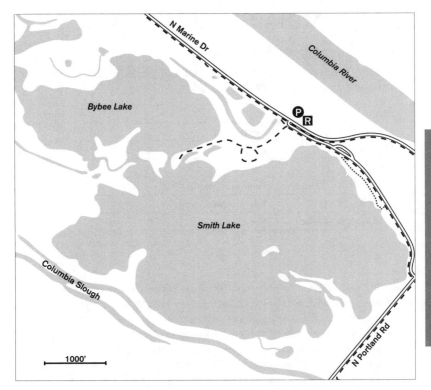

left-turning spur to a bird blind, where you can peer over the larger Smith Lake, and Turtle Turnout on the right, where you can see the famous western painted turtles sunning themselves. Back on the main trail you'll loop past a small pond and a meadow before ending at a covered shelter with a view of Bybee Lake.

On the return trek, you can continue down the 40-Mile Loop another 0.4 mile past the trailhead to reach a canoe launch for the wetlands. Here you can walk right down to the shore of Smith Lake. Late afternoons are especially magical, with the sight of the sun dipping toward the Tualatin Mountains and great blue herons flapping over colorful flotillas of kayakers.

ADDRESS: 5300 N Marine Drive, Portland

GETTING THERE: From I-5 N, take exit 307 for N Marine Drive, go 2.2 miles, and look for the trailhead on the left.

CONTACT: Metro, (503) 797-1545, oregonmetro.gov

<u>17</u> COLUMBIA SLOUGH TRAIL

7 miles north of downtown Portland

Walk along a paved dike path that curves alongside North Portland's secretive Columbia Slough.

TRAIL	4 miles
STEEPNESS	Gentle
OTHER USES	Bicycles
DOGS	On leash
CONNECTING TRAILS	Peninsula Crossing Trail
PARK AMENITIES	Interpretive displays
DISABLED ACCESS	Yes

North Portland's Kenton neighborhood provides walkers with access to Columbia Slough, a man-made 19-mile channel of water best known to area paddlers. An adventurous mind-set helps, as the walk begins from the Kenton / N Denver Avenue MAX Station and travels north on a pedestrian path for 0.3 mile across the busy Denver Avenue Viaduct. At the north end of the viaduct, Schmeer Road leads right to loop beneath the underpass, where signs for the Columbia Slough Trail lead the way west. (A 1.2-mile section of the slough trail, opened in 2014, extends to the east to Vancouver Avenue, but it's not as scenic.)

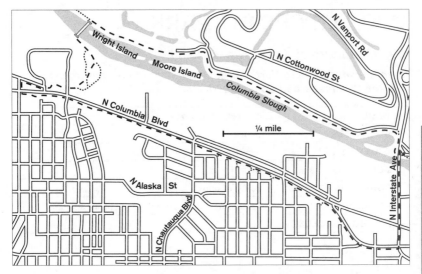

By 0.5 mile the expressway din is gone, and the slough's charm washes over you. Tall cottonwood trees screen out warehouses. Grasses dance in a breeze. Iridescent dragonflies whir like helicopters. Great blue herons stalk the water. Smartphone signals wane and silence reigns. Just to the north, you'll pass by Heron Lakes Golf Club, and at 1.8 miles you'll reach the Peninsula Crossing Bridge (a pedestrian bridge), where things get noisy. The largest concentration of cliff swallows in Portland roosts underneath and greets passersby with a chattery, acrobatic display.

On the bridge you can view anchored log rafts set in the brackish waters to boost fish habitat. Across the bridge, the Peninsula Crossing Trail starts in front of the Columbia Boulevard Wastewater Treatment Plant. Look for a series of stone steps etched with Columbia River flood-tide levels. These steps lead down to the water, providing a great vantage of the cliff-swallow nests. A short stretch continues by the treatment plant, where there's an interpretive path with nature-inspired art installations. But the most scenic option is to retrace your steps. (You can also follow the Peninsula Crossing Trail to N Columbia Boulevard and turn right on N Argyle Way for a straight shot back to the Kenton / N Denver Avenue MAX Station.)

ADDRESS: Kenton / N Denver Avenue MAX Station, 8319 N Denver Avenue, Portland

GETTING THERE: Arriving by MAX Light Rail (Kenton / N Denver Avenue stop) is the best option. Parking can be found at Kenton Park along N Brandon Avenue.

CONTACT: Columbia Slough Watershed Council, (503) 281-1132, columbiaslough.org

18 KELLEY POINT PARK

12.5 miles north of downtown Portland

Roam a leafy 104-acre North Portland park set at the convergence of the Willamette and Columbia Rivers.

TRAIL	Approximately 2 miles
STEEPNESS	Gentle
OTHER USES	Bicycles
DOGS	On leash
CONNECTING TRAILS	40-Mile Loop
PARK AMENITIES	Restrooms, interpretive displays, picnic shelters
DISABLED ACCESS	Yes

At its northern triangle-like tip, Kelley Point Park pokes into the confluence of the Willamette and Columbia Rivers. With its cottonwood-lined beaches and open, rolling lawns, it's one of Portland's most inviting (and egalitarian) parks.

Stroll here on any given day and you'll find hipsters sunning themselves on beaches, multiethnic families gathering around picnic tables, and maybe even a gaggle of larpers trotting into battle with foam swords and shields. (This *is* Portland, after all.) Luckily, with 104 acres and about 2 miles of paths, there's

plenty of room for everyone, not to mention a menagerie of wildlife.

Set out from the parking lot, and march right down to a sandy beach with smatterings of driftwood and views of the barge traffic on the river. Old pilings stretch out into the water, and your chances of seeing ospreys and double-breasted cormorants are good. Back on the main path, near a large shelter, you can set about circumnavigating the point, passing little spurs to more beaches. As the path winds, you'll reach a green central meadow surrounded by a large forest of black cottonwoods and maples that makes an attractive habitat for beavers, coyotes, and black-tailed deer.

At the northern tip of the park you can also stand before a large anchor marking the confluence of the rivers and get outstanding Mount Hood views. Along the way, interpretive signs inform visitors that during their first attempt to pinpoint the mouth of the Willamette in 1805, Lewis and Clark completely missed this point—certainly a mistake no Portlander should repeat.

ADDRESS: N Marine Drive and Lombard Street, Portland

GETTING THERE: From I-5 N, take exit 307 for N Marine Drive and drive approximately 6 miles, looking for the park entrance on the right. Continue to the second large parking lot at the end of the drive.

CONTACT: Portland Parks and Recreation, (503) 823-7529, portland oregon.gov/parks

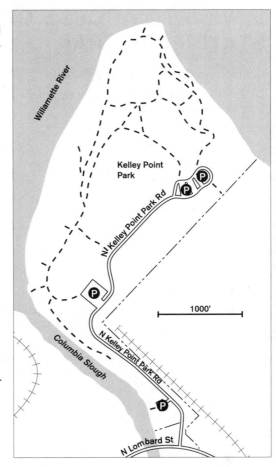

<u>19</u> WAPATO ACCESS GREENWAY STATE PARK TRAIL

14 miles north of downtown Portland

*Circle a forest-lined seasonal lake for outstanding
 birding opportunities.*

TRAIL	2-mile loop
STEEPNESS	Gentle
OTHER USES	Horses
DOGS	On leash
CONNECTING TRAILS	None
PARK AMENITIES	Bird blind, viewing platform, interpretive signs
DISABLED ACCESS	None

In contrast to more wide-open Sauvie Island spaces like Oak Island Trail (Walk #20), the Wapato Access Greenway State Park Trail provides a more intimate outing, circling the small seasonal Virginia Lake, which borders Multnomah Channel and is surrounded by dense stands of maples, red alders, and western hemlocks. Well-known to birders, the path is lined with a series of weathered wooden posts that identify commonly sighted birds and ducks, like pied-billed grebes, northern flickers, and willow flycatchers.

The trail starts on a wide gravel path that veers left past a picnic shelter. Here you can start the loop in either direction. Keep left to access a platform overlook-

ing the southern part of the wetland lake, and scan for beaver activity and arrow-shaped wapato, a staple food source for native peoples.

As the loop continues around the southern end of the lake, you'll pass a bird blind at 0.6 mile and then quickly come to a spur at Hadley's Landing, a boat dock in Multnomah Channel. The main path continues into a bottomland forest with thickets of alders. Rabbits scuttle about the trail, and garter snakes slither among the grasses. Look for a few fencepost-lined

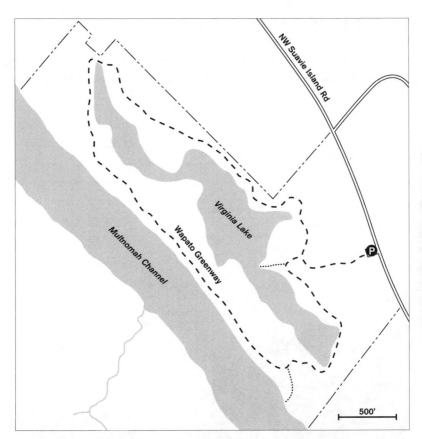

lookouts over the channel, where sunbaked old pilings act like snags, giving waterfowl a dry perch.

At 1.7 miles the canopy parts and the path crosses a wooden walkway at the northern tip of the lake. From here you'll duck under tall firs and large Oregon white oaks. In spring bushels of wild honeysuckle and roses scent the way on a gentle rise beside the lake before returning to the trailhead.

ADDRESS: Sauvie Island Road, Sauvie Island

GETTING THERE: From US 30 N, drive 10 miles to Sauvie Island, and turn right to cross the bridge. Follow NW Sauvie Island Road north for 3 miles, and look for the park on the left.

CONTACT: Oregon State Parks, (503) 986-0707, oregonstateparks.org

<u>20</u> OAK ISLAND TRAIL

Sauvie Island, 18 miles northwest of downtown Portland

Walk through oak savannahs to reach the edges of Sauvie Island's largest wetland lake.

TRAIL	2.4-mile loop
STEEPNESS	Gentle
OTHER USES	Pedestrians only
DOGS	On leash
CONNECTING TRAILS	None
PARK AMENITIES	Portable restroom
DISABLED ACCESS	None

  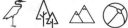

Set virtually in the middle of Sauvie Island's 24,000-acre expanse of rural farmland and state-managed wildlife areas, Oak Island appears like a scene from the PBS show *Nature*. Actually a peninsula, its oak-dotted savannahs are flanked by Steelman and Sturgeon Lakes, the latter being the largest lake on Sauvie Island.

A flat and easy loop (open April to September) traces the edge of the peninsula and comes with astounding wildlife viewing. The main path starts on double-track dirt road, past a hand-painted wooden sign and into a forest of Oregon white oaks full of chirping birds (white-breasted nuthatches are especially common).

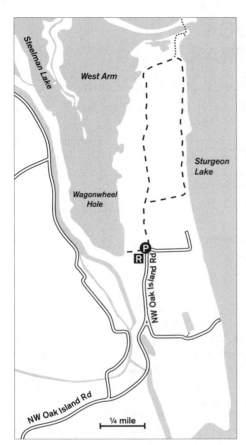

West Arm

Steelman Lake

Sturgeon Lake

Wagonwheel Hole

NW Oak Island Rd

NW Oak Island Rd

¼ mile

Past the forest you'll enter a wide grass prairie with free-range cattle and excellent views of the Tualatin Mountains. Yellow hiker signs help mark the start of the loop, which can be done in either direction.

Continue straight across the prairie and you'll skirt a fence line that protects nesting ground birds from April through July. At 1 mile, pass through a gate and follow the double-track road, which curves around a clump of trees to reveal another expanse of grassland and patches of wetlands. Search for egrets, herons, and bald eagles in this excellent setting. As you continue rounding this tip, look for a faint path heading to the left that leads to the Narrows, a thin arm of water that binds Steelman and Sturgeon Lakes.

Back on the main path, the 5,000-acre Sturgeon Lake comes into view, with sightlines of Mounts Saint Helens and Adams. At 2 miles you'll enter back into an oak canopy. With a large farm on the left, pass through another gate, returning to the main junction from the trailhead.

ADDRESS: Oak Island Road, Sauvie Island

GETTING THERE: From US 30 N, drive 10 miles to Sauvie Island and turn right to cross the bridge. Follow NW Sauvie Island Road north (left) for 2 miles. Turn right onto NW Reeder Road. Go 1 mile and turn left onto Oak Island Road. Go 3 miles and continue on an unpaved portion of road for 0.5 mile until you reach the trailhead. A Wildlife Area Parking Permit ($10) is required; they are available at the roadside store near the Sauvie Island Bridge.

CONTACT: Oregon Department of Fish and Wildlife, (503) 621-3488, dfw.state.or.us

21 WARRIOR ROCK LIGHTHOUSE TRAIL

Sauvie Island, 26 miles northwest of downtown Portland

Stroll along Columbia River beaches to reach one of the few remaining inland lighthouses in the country.

TRAIL	3.2 miles one way
STEEPNESS	Level
OTHER USES	Pedestrians only
DOGS	On leash
CONNECTING TRAILS	None
PARK AMENITIES	Portable restroom
DISABLED ACCESS	None

At just 28 feet tall, the white concrete edifice of the Warrior Rock Lighthouse is diminutive by lighthouse standards. But as one of only two remaining inland beacons in Oregon, Warrior Rock holds a high place in the state's seafaring lore. Set along the Columbia River at the northernmost tip of Sauvie Island, the original wooden structure was built in 1889. Replaced in the 1930s with concrete version, it was rebuilt in 1969 after a barge collided into it.

The trek to see this stubby but steadfast beacon is one of the most memorable walks around Portland. Following along a rutted and sometimes muddy road, you'll pass between a nearly continuous three-mile line of black cottonwood trees and the thin sandy beach along the Columbia River. The sounds of waves lapping against the shore and birds chattering fill the air, while billboard-size barges glide silently atop the river. At 0.6 mile a nice sandy cove is perfect for examining the expanse of the river. At 2.2 miles the lighthouse comes into view to the north, the sole inhabitant of this distant finger of land. Ahead the trail cuts through a large meadow and exits the woods into a sandy cove guarded by the lighthouse on the rock.

During salmon runs, the boat traffic on the river can be dizzying, with dozens of sport fisherman trying their luck.

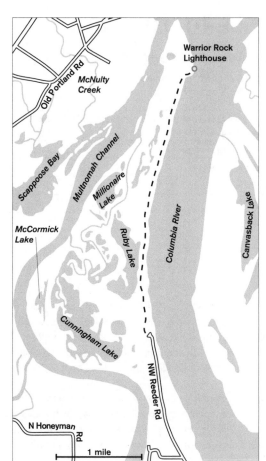

Careful eyes may also spot a hungry sea lion or two, bobbing along for fish as if attending a floating buffet. Across the river you can look directly over to Ridgefield National Wildlife Refuge (Walk #38). On sunny days the tip of the little beach brings views of Mount Saint Helens rising in the north.

ADDRESS: NW Reeder Road, Sauvie Island

GETTING THERE: From US 30 N, drive 10 miles and turn right to cross Sauvie Island Bridge. Follow NW Sauvie Island Road approximately 2 miles, and turn right onto NW Reeder Road. Go 6 miles. Reeder Road now becomes gravel. Continue 2 miles to the end of the road. A Wildlife Area Parking Permit ($10) is required; they are available at the small grocery store near the Sauvie Island Bridge.

CONTACT: Oregon Department of Fish and Wildlife, (503) 621-3488, dfw.state.or.us

22 CROWN ZELLERBACH TRAIL

Scappoose, 21 miles northwest of Portland

Leave the pavement behind on this little-known rail-to-trail path that rises into the wilds of the Coast Range.

TRAIL	22 miles total one way; approximately 3.5 miles one way as described here
STEEPNESS	Gentle to moderate
OTHER USES	Bicycles, horses
DOGS	On leash
CONNECTING TRAILS	None
PARK AMENITIES	None
DISABLED ACCESS	None

For the intrepid walker, the Crown Zellerbach (or CZ) Trail offers practically unlimited adventure. Like a feral version of the Banks-Vernonia State Trail (Walk #76), this remote-feeling old logging and railway passage dips, bends, and rises 22 mostly unpaved miles from the Multnomah Channel in Scappoose to the tiny logging town of Vernonia, cresting the Nehalem Divide summit (elevation 1,220 feet) in between.

Hacked out of the thick woods in spurts by the Portland & Southwestern Railroad during the 1900s, the rail line was morphed into a logging road by the Crown Zellerbach paper company in the 1940s and officially opened as a rail-to-trail path in 2013. The easiest access points line Scappoose Vernonia Highway, allowing walkers to try bite-size portions. The walk described here departs from the Chapman Grange Road trailhead, which sits between CZ mile points 9 and 10.

Most of the first mile parallels the highway, with road crossings at Chapman Grange Road, Chapman Road, and a small power station. Past mile marker 10,

near Rain Garden Lane, the trail breaks away from the road, descending into a particularly wild patch. Turning into a double-track trail around mile marker 11, the path curves through a gorgeous setting of cottonwoods, maples, alders, ferns, periwinkles, and wood sorrels, then dips down on a single track into an open gulley filled with yellow scotch broom. Then begin a slow rise to the Nehalem Divide

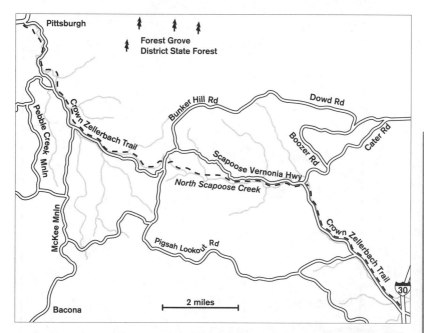

summit, looking for breaks in the canopy to the left, and you'll see wavelike crests of conifer-sided hills and feel Coast Range–born breezes rattling branches overhead. The trail continues, blazing through berms dense with sword ferns, imparting a canyon-like feel. Deer, elk, and even cougar sightings are a very real possibility.

By mile marker 13, the forest becomes dusky and lush as it wraps above a pair of steep brush-shrouded gullies before curving back beneath Scappoose Vernonia Highway under a bridge. To the left you can exit the trail onto the gravel Pisgah Lookout Road (an alternate trailhead).

The trail continues beneath the underpass, dropping steeply into even wilder brush, though a lack of signage, multiple logging-road intersections, and the prospect of an uphill return make the bridge a good turnaround point.

ADDRESS: Scappoose Vernonia Highway and Chapman Grange Road, Scappoose

GETTING THERE: From US 30 N, drive 21 miles to Scappoose. Turn left onto Scappoose Vernonia Highway, go approximately 6 miles (passing a well-signposted CZ trailhead at 1.8 miles on the right, across from the B&B Market), and look for a large gravel lot on the left, also signposted for the CZ Trail, just before Chapman Grange Road.

CONTACT: Columbia County Forests, Parks, and Recreation, (503) 397-2353, co.columbia.or.us

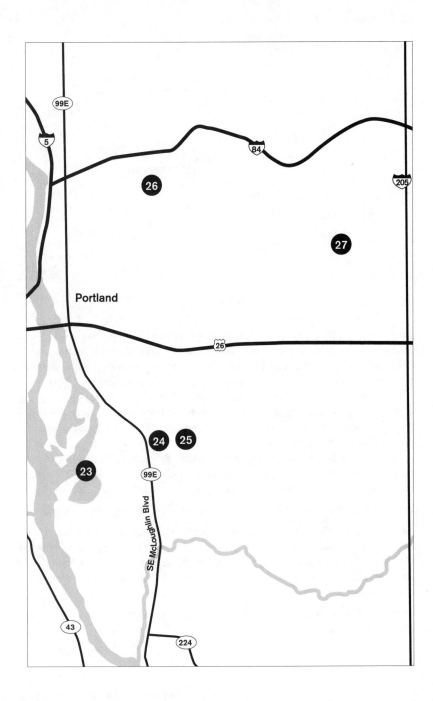

SE PORTLAND

SOUTHEAST PORTLAND

23 OAKS BOTTOM WILDLIFE REFUGE

3 miles southeast of downtown Portland

This Audubon Society Important Bird Area lets walkers take flight in the heart of the city.

TRAIL	2.4 miles
STEEPNESS	Gentle, with one steep portion on return
OTHER USES	Bicycles on Springwater Corridor
DOGS	On leash
CONNECTING TRAILS	Springwater Corridor
PARK AMENITIES	None
DISABLED ACCESS	None

It's difficult to overstate Oaks Bottom Wildlife Refuge's status as a symbol of Portland's green beating heart. In 1988 this 168-acre marshland along the eastern banks of the Willamette River, just 10 minutes from downtown, became the city's first urban wildlife refuge. The Springwater Corridor, Portland's signature greenway, leads straight to the park's edge. The town's

official bird, the great blue heron (along with 185 other species of birds), gathers by the dozens, garnering Oaks Bottom a designation as an Audubon Society Important Bird Area.

Start from Sellwood Park, which lines a bluff just south of the refuge. An interpretive panel marks a rocky path that drops to a large meadow at the south end of the refuge. On the right, a one-mile trail borders the base of the bluff, leading into a seam of black cottonwoods, maples, ash, and willows. Sticking to the left of the meadow, walkers can reach the Springwater Corridor via a pedestrian underpass connecting to the venerable Oaks Park. This portion of the Springwater Corridor parallels railroad tracks and gains an elevated look over the refuge's central lake. Herons seem omnipresent, croaking and gouging the muddy shallows with their beaks. Sunlight glistens on the Willamette River to the left and illuminates the famous mural adorning Wilhelm's Portland Memorial Mausoleum, which juts out of the trees above Oaks Bottom. (Measuring 55,000 square feet and filled with depictions of refuge birdlife, it's as much an icon as the park itself.)

About 0.5 mile up the Springwater Corridor, a second pedestrian underpass connects walkers to a trail leading back under the bluff. At 1.5 miles you'll duck directly beneath the mausoleum's megasized art and arrive at a large observation platform near the lake. Just ahead, the trail meets meadow and climbs back to Sellwood Park. The platform is a great place to linger as the sun dips below the West Hills and fleeting rays catch the wings of herons and egrets floating above the refuge.

ADDRESS: SE 7th Ave and Sellwood Boulevard, Portland

GETTING THERE: From the Sellwood Bridge in Portland, turn onto SE 7th Avenue and park at the north end of the Sellwood Park parking lot.

CONTACT: Portland Parks and Recreation, (503) 823-7529, portlandoregon.gov/parks

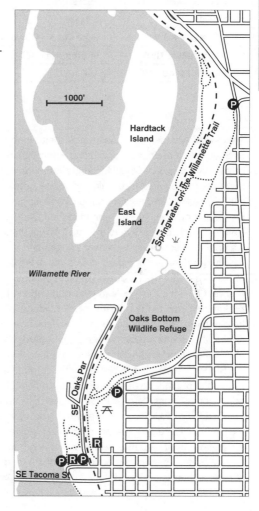

24 CRYSTAL SPRINGS RHODODENDRON GARDEN

3 miles southeast of downtown Portland

One of Portland's most scenic gardens is filled with fragrant flowers.

TRAIL	Up to 1 mile
STEEPNESS	Gentle
OTHER USES	Pedestrians only
DOGS	On leash
CONNECTING TRAILS	Reed College Canyon (Walk #25)
PARK AMENITIES	Interpretive displays, restrooms
DISABLED ACCESS	Yes

They come with names as colorful as their blooms: Tally Ho. Holy Moses. Queen of Sheba. And at peak bloom during April and May, the two thousand rhododendrons and azaleas of Crystal Springs Rhododendron Garden ignite a staggering blaze of puffy orange, red, pink, and yellow petals.

Opened in 1950 as a rhododendron test garden, these 7 acres sit between the august grounds of Eastmoreland Golf Course and Reed College in Southeast Portland, and have grown to include 140 varieties of trees as well as lagoons and waterfalls, all accessed by ornate bridges and curving gravel paths.

The gardens are hemmed in on three sides by Crystal Springs Lake, a shallow pool fed by more than a dozen burbling springs. The waters divide the space into two sections: the Peninsula to the north and the Island to the south. A boardwalk bridge connects the two spaces. Self-guided walking-tour maps are available and help detail subtle features, such as unusual tree varieties like the dawn redwood, a conifer that sheds needles in winter, or a garden wall hewn from stones gathered on Mounts Hood and Adams in the 1950s.

But there's no need to pick a particular route—any flight of fancy will do. (Do expect the grounds to be crowded at the height of bloom season. There is a $4 admission fee from March 1 through Labor Day, except on Mondays and Tuesdays.)

An array of birdlife means that the bright colors extend well beyond the spring blossoms. Volunteers have recorded seventy-nine avian species in the garden. Birds are particularly abundant in winter. With the grounds all but deserted by humans, Crystal Springs becomes a boutique birdbath for ducks, geese, and gulls. Gaggles of quacking mallards, wood ducks, ruddy ducks, American wigeons, lesser scaups, and buffleheads congregate at your feet (many looking for a handout, which is not

encouraged), making for a slow but highly endearing stroll.

ADDRESS: 6015 SE 28th Avenue, Portland

GETTING THERE: From OR 99 E / SE McLoughlin Boulevard in Southeast Portland, head south. Take a slight right onto SE 23rd Avenue and then turn left on SE Bybee Boulevard. Continue on SE Tolman Street, then take a quick left onto SE 28th Avenue and look for the gardens on the left.

CONTACT: (503) 771-8386, crystal-springsgarden.org; Portland Parks and Recreation, (503) 823-7529, portland oregon.gov/parks

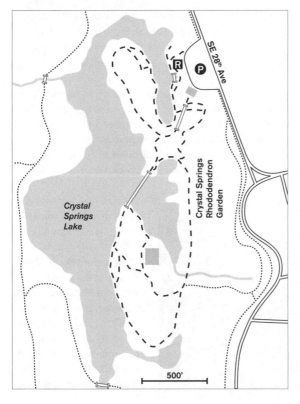

<u>25</u> REED COLLEGE CANYON

5 miles southeast of downtown Portland

A stately Southeast Portland college campus doubles as a 15-acre wildlife refuge.

TRAIL	1 mile
STEEPNESS	Gentle
OTHER USES	Students studying
DOGS	On leash
CONNECTING TRAILS	Crystal Springs Rhododendron Garden (Walk #24)
PARK AMENITIES	None
DISABLED ACCESS	None

Did you hear the one about the osprey that ate someone's homework? Well, it seems plausible on the campus of Reed College. Smack in the middle of this manicured redbrick campus, you'll discover what feels like the country's largest biology class—a 15-acre forested canyon lake that's been designated as an official state wildlife refuge.

Reed Lake, which is thought to be the oldest naturally occurring lake in Portland, serves as the headwaters for Crystal Springs Creek. The stream drains the lake from east to west and, with the aid of a fish ladder, supports a population of coho salmon, rainbow trout, lamprey, and other gilled inhabitants. More than eighty bird species have been observed utilizing the generous cover of maples, western red cedars, black locusts, and red alders, along with a jumble of snags and stumps in the lake.

And while students do study the canyon intensely (setting up cameras to confirm beaver activity and writing papers like "Salmon Increase in the Reed Canyon: A Multi-Year Study of Conservation and Restoration"), all you need to do is wander the easy 1-mile loop trail. From the lower end of SE Botsford Drive, near SE 28th Avenue, wooden steps drop down along the rushing creek waters. Boardwalks link to wood-chip paths that track both edges of the canyon. Either side will funnel you along an understory of salmonberry, jewelweed, and common horsetail toward a small gurgling waterfall, then beneath a pair of bridges and the wooded lake edges.

At the western rim, all signs of campus disappear amid marsh habitat brimming with egrets, herons, and belted kingfishers. On the loop back, head up either side of the central bridge (set between Bragdon Hall and Eliot Hall) for a jaw-dropping vantage directly over the lake.

ADDRESS: SE Botsford Drive and SE 28th Avenue, Portland

GETTING THERE: From downtown, cross the Hawthorne Bridge and follow SE Hawthorne Boulevard east to César E. Chávez Boulevard. Turn right and go 3.5 miles to SE Woodstock Boulevard. Continue to SE 28th Avenue and turn right. Take the Botsford Drive entrance on the right and park at the Performing Arts Building.

CONTACT: Reed College, (503) 771-1112, reed.edu

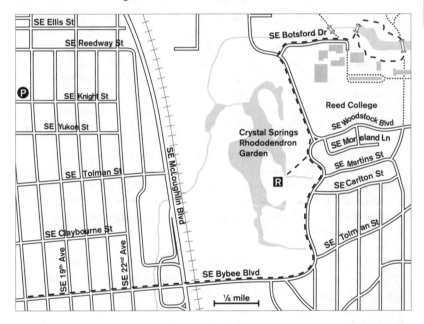

26 LONE FIR CEMETERY

2 miles east of downtown Portland

This Southeast Portland cemetery sits beneath one of the largest tree canopies in the city and is filled with chirping bird life.

TRAIL	1 mile
STEEPNESS	Gentle
OTHER USES	Bicycles, automobiles
DOGS	Not allowed
CONNECTING TRAILS	None
PARK AMENITIES	Monthly guided walking tours; self-guided tour information is available online
DISABLED ACCESS	Yes

Lone Fir is Portland's largest historic pioneer cemetery, with twenty-five thousand plots, the oldest dating to 1846. But to leaf- and bark-obsessed walkers, it's more like an arboreal cathedral. The 30 acres, now maintained as a Metro park property, fill a rectangle in the city's Central Eastside with more than seven hundred trees spanning sixty-seven unique varieties. Dogwoods, ginkgoes, birches, sequoias, black locusts (an especially cemetery-worthy candidate, with its dark, distorted limbs)—the diverse assemblage is surpassed only by Hoyt Arboretum (Walk #1). Birders will also tell you that the grounds serve as a location for the Audubon Society of Portland's annual species counts.

Tracing the paved perimeter paths paralleling SE Stark Street and SE Morrison Street nets about a mile of walking. The interior lanes add more distance and are especially peaceful. (Cars are allowed, but drivers keep a respectful speed, and walkers rule the day.) With so many trees, you can't go wrong. Stroller pushers, photographers, canoodling picnickers, and readers enjoy every corner of this green space. Most outings begin on the east side, at an open gate on SE 26th Avenue, where there's plenty of parking.

A ramble to find the cemetery's three Heritage Trees (trees recognized by the city council as unique for their size, age, historical, or horticultural significance), including the original namesake fir, is a fun way to fill an hour or two. There's the General Joseph Lane tree, an immense big-leaf maple planted to honor one of Oregon's first US senators (the

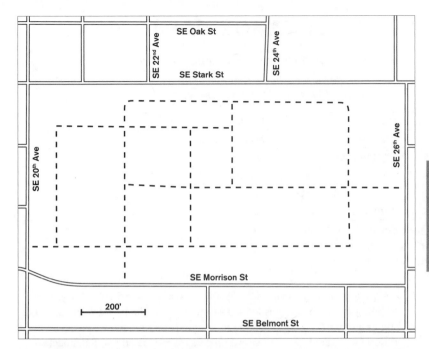

small memorial plaque is now slowly being pushed aside by the tree's kraken-like roots), and a 100-foot incense cedar resembling a Q-tip the Jolly Green Giant might need. The Lone Fir, an 85-foot whopper, stands in the northwest corner near the Firemen's Cemetery area.

Headstone sleuthing is very popular. You'll likely recognize several names, like that of Asa Lovejoy, the famous cofounder of Portland who lost a coin flip to name the city "Boston." Or Socrates Tryon, who Tryon Creek State Natural Area (Walk #10) was named for. In the southwest corner of the cemetery, there are plans for a new heritage garden that will commemorate an unheralded population of Chinese workers as well a compassionate doctor who ran a nearby pioneer-era asylum—many of the good doctor's patients are buried here.

Self-guided tour information (available online at friendsoflonefircemetery.org) is well worth keeping handy to pinpoint other notable residents. Mark your calendar for the cemetery's beloved Halloween Tour of Untimely Departures. These candlelit events feature costumed actors embodying the ghosts of a few Lone Fir souls that met unfortunate ends long ago.

ADDRESS: SE 26th Avenue and SE Washington Street, Portland

GETTING THERE: From the Morrison Bridge, travel east on SE Belmont Street and turn left onto SE 26th Avenue.

CONTACT: Metro, (503) 797-1709, oregonmetro.gov

27 MOUNT TABOR PARK

3.5 miles east of downtown Portland

Spectacular views atop this extinct volcano come with enormous trees, a broad lawn, and historic reservoirs.

TRAIL	Up to 9 miles
STEEPNESS	Moderate to steep
OTHER USES	Bicycles
DOGS	On leash
CONNECTING TRAILS	None
PARK AMENITIES	Restrooms, playgrounds, dog park
DISABLED ACCESS	Yes

You've got to love a park that's actually a volcano in the middle of the city. Topping out at 643 feet, Mount Tabor is indeed a 3-million-year-old extinct volcano, and its hulking tree-topped slopes form a green backbone on Portland's east side.

Paved paths, dirt trails, stairways, and park roads lace around the mountain, winding amid 190 acres' worth of wondrously tall trees, historic open-air reservoirs, and a summit with the city's best sunset views, hands down. You could easily spend the better part of a day exploring here. But prep your glutes for some hill walking, as almost every path goes up.

Maps at the park's visitor center and information kiosk help you dial in a comfortable amount of climbing. You'll find three well-signposted, color-coded walk options. The 1-mile Red Trail and the 1.7-mile Green Trail are the tamest, sticking mainly to lower paved trails and roads. The best

views—and workouts—come from the 3-mile Blue Trail, a virtual Tour de Tabor that drops into a shady ravine, ascends ninety-five steep steps, and visits all three iconic reservoirs, which, up until 2015, held millions of gallons of the city's drinking water. Now disconnected to comply with federal mandates, these basins still serve as enormous reflecting pools and are guarded by photogenic castle-like turrets.

There is no bad time to visit. With nearly sixty different kinds of trees, and rhododendrons, camellias, and orb-like hydrangeas sprinkled throughout, something is perpetually

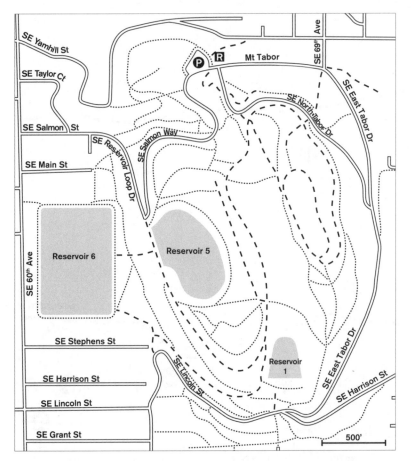

in bloom. Birders also swear by the spring migration here. And take note: each Wednesday all park roads are closed to car traffic, making it a particularly good day for walking.

If you'd rather just visit the summit, head to the stairs at the 69th Avenue entrance. An attraction in its own right, this flight climbs 282 calf-chiseling steps beneath gigantic Douglas firs and maples to the top. Here you can trace a 0.3-mile loop on a closed road and catch the late-day rays glinting off downtown high-rises beneath the rugged West Hills.

ADDRESS: SE 69th Avenue and SE Yamhill Street, Portland

GETTING THERE: From downtown Portland, take the Morrison Bridge and continue on SE Belmont Street for 3 miles to SE 69th Avenue. Turn right and then keep right on the park drive, following the sign for the volcano lot.

CONTACT: Portland Parks and Recreation, (503) 823-7529, portlandoregon.gov/parks

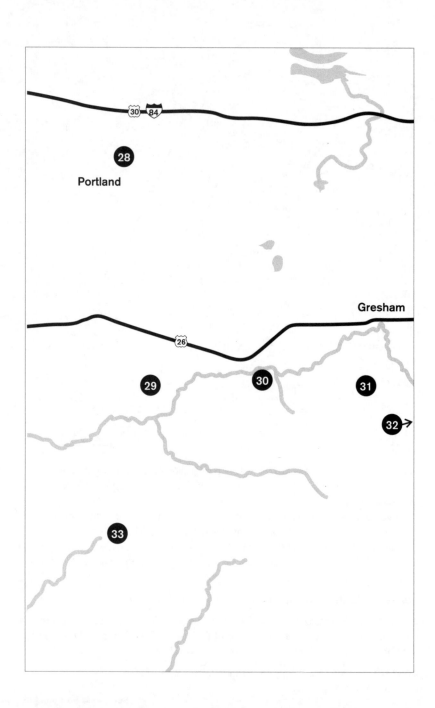

EAST PORTLAND & GRESHAM

<u>28</u> GLENDOVEER FITNESS TRAIL

10 miles east of downtown Portland

A wood-chip trail encircling Glendoveer Golf Course provides throwback-style fitness.

TRAIL	2.2-mile loop
STEEPNESS	Gentle
OTHER USES	Pedestrians only
DOGS	Not allowed
CONNECTING TRAILS	None
PARK AMENITIES	Restrooms
DISABLED ACCESS	None

The old adage claims that golf is a good walk spoiled—not so on this immaculate 2.2-mile wood-chip trail wrapping around Glendoveer Golf Course in Northeast Portland. Composed of two eighteen-hole courses, the grounds date to 1924 and are blessed with characteristic Pacific Northwest good looks. Storybook stands of Douglas firs, sequoias, and cedars bookend fairways, making the greens appear like lush mountain meadows. Far from stuffy, Glendoveer, now administered by Metro, has long been described as the kind of place you'd see your mail carrier working on his short game. That kind of everybody-knows-your-name vibe extends to the beloved fitness path.

Walk here and you'll join a merry-go-round of chipper regulars. Older gentlemen breaking in knee replacements. Speedy Fitbit-checking runners. New moms with sleeping babes strapped on their chests. Pairs of elderly ladies tossing seeds to squirrels, as they have for years (even though nowadays signs discourage this). And *everyone* smiles, nods, or says hello.

If that's not charming enough, the scenery is first-rate. Long woodsy corridors line the eastern and western edges the course, rising above a bevy of bright flowers. Blooms occur year-round, from blue violets and periwinkles in February to wild grapes and bittersweet nightshade in July and August. You might encounter other inhabitants, like rufous hummingbirds, western screech owls, or urban coyotes.

A dedicated walking trailhead at NE 148th Avenue and NE Halsey Street makes it easy to tackle the route in a clockwise or counterclockwise loop. (Plenty of regulars do both.) But to get the traffic-heavy stretch along NE Glisan Street over with, head clockwise on an uphill track through gorgeous Douglas firs and thimbleberries. Rounding a silver water tower, the 0.5-mile stretch along busy NE Glisan goes by quick.

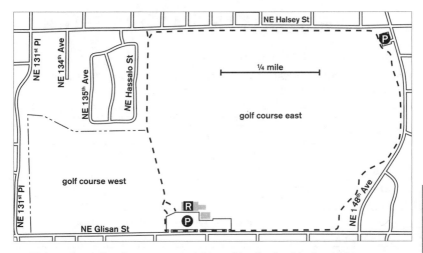

NE Halsey St

NE 131st Pl
NE 134th Ave
NE 135th Ave
NE Hassalo St

¼ mile

golf course east

golf course west

NE 131st Pl

NE 148th Ave

NE Glisan St

Pick up the trail at the west end of the parking lot, beside the driving range, and descend into the quietest segment of the course. Rounding the corner on NE Halsey Street, the homestretch is lined with colossal blue spruces, western red cedars, giant sequoias, and a 145-foot Douglas fir marked as an official Portland Heritage Tree.

ADDRESS: NE 148th Avenue and NE Halsey Street, Portland

GETTING THERE: From I-84 E, take exit 6 for I-205 S. Follow signs for Glisan Street / Stark Street, and turn left onto NE Glisan Street. Drive 2 miles and turn left onto NE 148th Avenue. Go 0.4 mile and look for the trailhead on the left, just before NE Halsey Street.

CONTACT: Metro, (503) 665-4995, oregonmetro.gov; Glendoveer Golf Course, (503) 253-7507, play glendoveer.com

<u>29</u> POWELL BUTTE NATURE PARK

9 miles southeast of downtown Portland

One of Portland's largest natural areas comprises over 600 acres of meadow and forest.

TRAIL	Up to 8 miles; 2.1-mile loop as described here
STEEPNESS	Gentle to moderate
OTHER USES	Mountain bikes, horses
DOGS	On leash
CONNECTING TRAILS	Springwater Corridor
PARK AMENITIES	Visitor center, restrooms, interpretive displays, artwork
DISABLED ACCESS	Yes

At 611 acres, the mighty Powell Butte Nature Park ranks as Southeast Portland's largest open space, encompassing vast meadowlands trimmed by steep flanks of Douglas firs and western red cedars. The 630-foot rise gets breezes funneled in from the Columbia River Gorge that rustle through the historic orchard and a tallgrass prairie—which affords majestic Mount Hood views. Long used as an underground reservoir site for Portland's water supply, the butte's tranquility was interrupted in 2015 by an extensive construction effort to bury a new 50-million-gallon storage tank. Now that the work is completed, the butte's peaceful spirit is back, and the park has a sleek new visitor center (open Wednesday through Sunday) and refurbished trails.

With 8 miles of paths, walk options abound, including a link to the Springwater Corridor, which zips below the park's southern border. From the visitor center, which features a wall-sized aerial photograph of the park, and shiny art installa-

tions evoking the reservoir pipes, you can take the popular paved Mountain View Trail. In just 0.5 mile, this gently climbing path visits the butte's old orchard of walnut, pear, and apple trees and the redesigned Mountain Finder. Here angular steel markers point out every significant peak and butte in the Portland area–ten in all–from Mount Jefferson in the south to Mount Saint Helens in the north.

Just ahead, the crushed-gravel Summit Lane borders a wooden fence with sightlines of Mount Hood framed by a series of wooded buttes. Summit Lane then wraps north up a gentle incline overlooking a pair of ponds set in a grassy meadow. Take time to scan for raptors like the American kestrel along this stretch. As the path rises, you'll spot the orchard again and pass connector trails, like the Hawthorn and Douglas Fir Trails, that drop down into the forest. Keep right to find your way back to the Mountain View Trail and the parking lot.

ADDRESS: 16160 SE Powell Boulevard, Portland

GETTING THERE: From I-205 S, take exit 19 for SE Division and turn left. Drive 2 miles and turn right (south) on SE 136th Avenue. Continue 0.4 mile to SE Powell Boulevard. Turn left and go approximately 1 mile to the park entrance on the right.

CONTACT: Portland Parks and Recreation, 503-823-7529, portlandoregon.gov /parks; Friends of Powell Butte Nature Park, friendsofpowellbutte.org

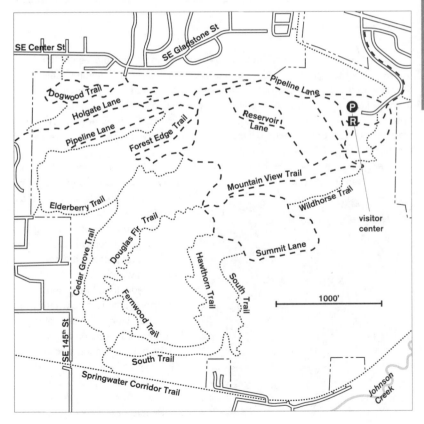

30 BUTLER CREEK GREENWAY TRAIL

Gresham, 12 miles east of downtown Portland

*A surprisingly wild greenway path is hidden between the
Springwater Corridor and Gresham's Butler Creek Park.*

TRAIL	2.8 miles round-trip
STEEPNESS	Gentle
OTHER USES	Bicycles on Springwater Corridor
DOGS	On leash
CONNECTING TRAILS	Springwater Corridor
PARK AMENITIES	Restrooms, paved trails
DISABLED ACCESS	Springwater Corridor

Just east of Powell Butte, the Gresham Woods provide a dense green buffer
between the Springwater Corridor and the rushing waters of Johnson Creek. The
40 acres of willows, cottonwoods, and western red cedars host an array of songbirds and raptors, along with amphibians like Pacific tree frogs and rough-skinned
newts. Consider it a scenic front doorstep to the Butler Creek Greenway Trail,
which dips south from Gresham Woods through a furtive neighborhood glen to
the green lawns of Butler Creek Park.

The Springwater Corridor's Linnemann Station Trailhead—a former rail hub for
the interurban line that began running in 1903—provides easy access to Gresham

Woods. From the station it's just a
0.2-mile walk east to the junction
with the greenway, which plunges
south into the Gresham Woods on
a wide gravel path. At the south
end of the woods, a 135-foot-long
arched pedestrian bridge fords
rushing Johnson Creek, where you
might see black-tailed deer along
the banks or herons on the wing.

The path continues across SW
14th Drive and into a deepening
forest that fronts Butler Creek, a
tributary of Johnson Creek. Along
SW Binford Lake Parkway, the trail

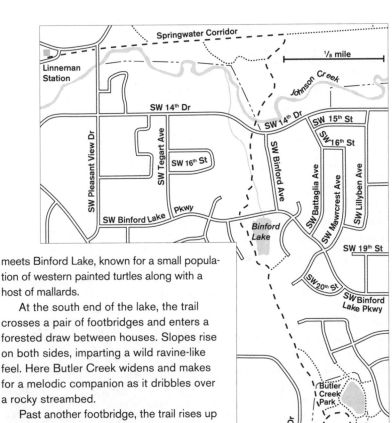

meets Binford Lake, known for a small population of western painted turtles along with a host of mallards.

At the south end of the lake, the trail crosses a pair of footbridges and enters a forested draw between houses. Slopes rise on both sides, imparting a wild ravine-like feel. Here Butler Creek widens and makes for a melodic companion as it dribbles over a rocky streambed.

Past another footbridge, the trail rises up above the creek, which tumbles down in a miniature cascade from Butler Creek Park. Inside the park, a disc-golf course, wide lawns, and a series of paved paths provide plenty of reason to linger before retracing your steps back.

ADDRESS: *Linneman Station:* 3804 W Powell Loop, Gresham; *Butler Creek Park:* 2385 SW 27th Drive, Gresham

GETTING THERE: Follow SE Powell Boulevard to Gresham, turn right onto W Powell Loop, and look for the Linnemann Station Trailhead parking on the left. The Springwater Corridor is directly behind the trailhead parking.

CONTACT: Gresham Parks and Recreation, (503) 618-2300, greshamoregon.gov/parks

31 GRESHAM BUTTE SADDLE TRAIL

Gresham, 14 miles east of downtown Portland

Old logging paths explore the hilly terrain of Gresham's largest natural area.

TRAIL	1.2 miles one way
STEEPNESS	Moderate
OTHER USES	Bicycles
DOGS	On leash
CONNECTING TRAILS	Springwater Corridor
PARK AMENITIES	None
DISABLED ACCESS	None

Reminiscent of the kind of rugged fire-lane roads lacing through Forest Park, the Gresham Butte Saddle Trail splits between a pair of heavily forested mounds on the undulating track of an old logging road. The buttes—Gresham Butte to the north and Gabbert Hill to the south—are just two of nine extinct volcanic domes within the city limits, all of which are part of the larger pre-historic Boring Lava Field stretching through the east side of the metro area.

The wide track travels west–east and is lined with a forest of Douglas firs and large maples. Salals, vine maples, sword ferns, and remnants of an old holly plantation add a lush understory, and a low hand-cobbled rock wall lines several portions of the trail. At 0.6 mile the trail reaches a four-way junction in the middle of the saddle.

A lone interpretive sign describes the rare Hogan western red cedar, which grows only in Gresham. This variety displays a highly symmetrical pyramid shape, and its origin is a mystery. (A grove of Hogans sits about a mile away, on the eastern edges of Gresham Butte near Hogan Road and Johnson Creek.) A desire to preserve these trees played a large role in motivating protestors in the 1970s to battle the proposed Mount Hood Freeway, which would have cut through the area.

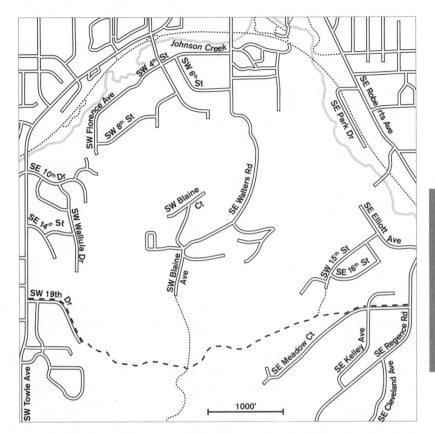

From this four-way junction, walkers up for a challenge can climb a brutally steep path up Gabbert Hill to the right, which leads to a water tower and an abandoned bus from the Mount Hood Freeway project days. If you keep straight at the junction, the path dips along a rock wall and breaks out of the canopy near SE Meadow Court and SE 19th Street. Here you can scan the open canopy for raptors before turning back. (Walkers can also link to the Springwater Corridor by following SE 19th Street to SE Regner Road and heading north for 0.4 mile.)

ADDRESS: SW Towle Avenue and SW 19th Drive, Gresham

GETTING THERE: Follow SE Powell Boulevard to Gresham and turn right on SW Towle Avenue. Turn right onto Eastman Parkway, which becomes SW Towle Avenue. Turn left onto SW 19th Drive and look for the trailhead at the end of a cul-de-sac.

CONTACT: Gresham Parks and Recreation, (503) 618-6300, greshamoregon.gov/parks

<u>32</u> OXBOW REGIONAL PARK

Troutdale, 20 miles east of Portland

Admire the largest grove of old-growth forest in the Portland metro area, and view the banks of the Sandy River.

TRAIL	Up to 12 miles; 4 miles as described here
STEEPNESS	Moderate to steep
OTHER USES	Horses
DOGS	Not allowed
CONNECTING TRAILS	None
PARK AMENITIES	Restrooms, water, picnic areas, campgrounds, play areas, nature programs
DISABLED ACCESS	None

Named for characteristic U-shaped bows within the Sandy River Gorge, 1,200-acre Oxbow Regional Park and its full-service campground deliver a deep-woods experience within 40 minutes of town.

Twelve miles of trails access the biggest concentration of old-growth trees near Portland, a high ridgetop meadow known to attract Roosevelt elk, and long ridgelines that survey the Sandy River, which is federally designated as a Wild and Scenic River. Maps are available at the entrance gate and are indispensable—the gorge can be disorienting. It's helpful to note that trails are encountered in alphabetical order, from Trail A to Trail O, as you drive down the main park road.

Trail A starts 0.1 mile beyond the entrance gate, off a small unpaved picnic loop, and serves as a good leg warmer on the way to the ancient forest. The rolling

track parallels the park road for just shy of a mile and then joins Trail B to enter into the 160-acre grove of old-growth forest. (A small parking area in the Happy Creek Day Area about a mile from the entrance gate also provides access to Trail B.)

Beneath the supersized stands of Douglas firs, some estimated at 700 years old, tall white blooms of cow

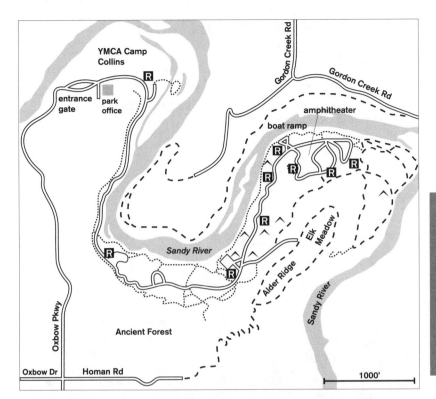

parsnip and paper-lantern-like Columbia lilies contrast the deep greens of moss and ferns. Salmonberries and Pacific red elderberries bloom profusely. Following the signs for the E, F, and G trails, you can access a 1-mile loop around Alder Ridge and Elk Meadow, but it requires a steep climb up a gravel road.

For a look at the Sandy River, descend Trail D in the center of the ancient forest and cross over the park road. Turn right on Trail C, and you'll come to a group picnic shelter area. A 0.5-mile trail overlooks the green waters set below layers of cottonwoods and firs. In fall it's possible to spot wild Chinook salmon flopping in the shallows as they spawn.

ADDRESS: 3010 SE Oxbow Parkway, Gresham

GETTING THERE: From I-84 E, take exit 17 for Troutdale. Follow the frontage road and turn right onto SW 257th Avenue. Go approximately 3 miles and turn left onto SE Division Street. Go 2.7 miles and head right on Oxbow Drive. Go 2.3 miles and turn left onto Oxbow Parkway. Continue to the park entrance (a $5 day pass is required).

CONTACT: Metro, (503) 663-4708, oregonmetro.gov

<u>33</u> SCOUTERS MOUNTAIN NATURE PARK

Happy Valley, 15 miles southeast of downtown Portland

This new 100-acre park rings the top of a 932-foot-tall lava dome with stunning views of Mount Hood.

TRAIL	1.2 miles
STEEPNESS	Moderate
OTHER USES	Pedestrians only
DOGS	Not allowed
CONNECTING TRAILS	None
PARK AMENITIES	Restrooms, group picnic shelter, interpretive signs
DISABLED ACCESS	Yes

Once the site of a long-lived Boy Scout camp, Scouters Mountain near Happy Valley seems destined to continue a long tradition of nurturing love for the outdoors. The 932-foot-tall extinct lava dome is a natural site for exploration, with panoramic Cascade Range views and stands of centuries-old Douglas firs. After several years of restoration work, Metro opened the 100-acre site in 2014, with about 1.2 miles of freshly minted trails to walk.

The ADA-compliant Shelter Trail leads up from the main parking lot into a stand of impressive Douglas firs and up to the Lava Dome Trail, which circles the top of the mountain. Clear days mean unrivaled views of Mount Hound and glimpses over the Columbia River and into Washington. During windy, drizzly outings, the sturdy picnic shelter atop the peak

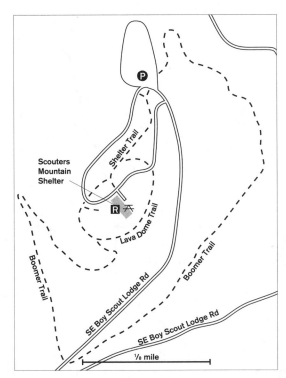

Scouters Mountain Shelter

Shelter Trail

Lava Dome Trail

Boomer Trail

Boomer Trail

SE Boy Scout Lodge Rd

SE Boy Scout Lodge Rd

⅛ mile

is especially welcoming. Exposed wooden beams and stones within the shelter were salvaged from the Boy Scouts' Chief Obie Lodge, which occupied the area from 1952 to 2004. (A series of benches in the park also features reused old-growth lumber from the Boy Scout lodge.)

After circling the summit, trace the Boomer Trail down into a deep forest of Douglas firs and maples clinging to the mountainside. (The trail is named for an unusual species of mountain beaver that lives here.) As the trail continues through the mountain's lush eastern flanks, scan the forest floor for mushrooms and herds of black-tailed deer silently loping among the trees before you loop back to the trailhead.

And if the outing ends too soon for you, take note: long-term plans for the park include a 34-mile loop trail linking to the Springwater Corridor, Powell Butte, and Mount Scott.

ADDRESS: SE 147 Avenue and SE Boy Scout Lodge Road, Happy Valley

GETTING THERE: From I-205 S take exit 17 for SE Foster Road and keep left onto SE Foster Road. Go 0.6 mile, turn right onto SE 110th Avenue, and continue straight on SE 112th Avenue. Continue onto SE Mount Scott Boulevard, then continue on SE King Road for 0.8 mile and turn right onto SE 145th Avenue. Look for a park sign, turn left onto SE Boy Scout Lodge Road, and follow signs to the parking lot.

CONTACT: Metro, (503) 665-4995, oregonmetro.gov

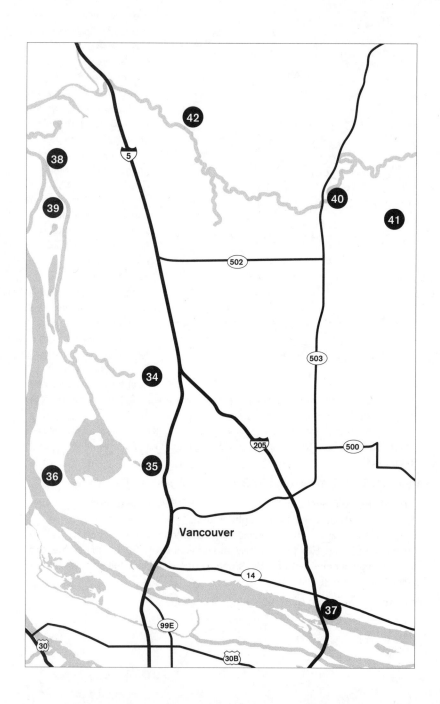

VANCOUVER, WASHINGTON

<u>34</u> SALMON CREEK GREENWAY TRAIL

Vancouver, WA, 14.5 miles north of downtown Portland

Walk a paved 3-mile wetland trail blessed with mountain views and outstanding wildlife.

TRAIL	3.1 miles one way; 6.2 miles round-trip
STEEPNESS	Gentle (with two moderate sections)
OTHER USES	Bicycles, horses
DOGS	On leash (not allowed over bridge to Klineline Pond)
CONNECTING TRAILS	Cougar Creek Trail
PARK AMENITIES	Restrooms, sports fields, spray park, fishing
DISABLED ACCESS	Yes

Draining a 90-square-mile watershed in central Clark County, Salmon Creek maintains a tidal link via its confluence with Lake River to the west, which in turn empties into the Columbia River, which finally mixes with the Pacific Ocean. That's a long way of saying that yes, there are indeed salmon in Salmon Creek. (A small population of migrating winter steelhead to be exact.) For now. This highly urban watershed has been named one of Washington's ten most endangered habitats. And a visit along its namesake 3-mile paved greenway reveals that it's well worth appreciating.

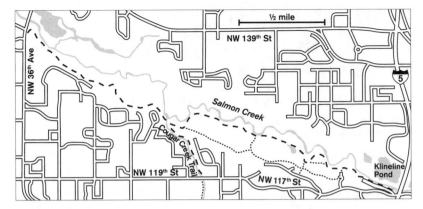

Reed-filled marshes, creeks, and ponds, as well as densely forested inclines clustered with Indian plums, vine maples, and firs, amass like a green halo along the shoreline that makes up the Salmon Creek Greenway Trail. Access comes easy, and the trail is nearly level, making it a favorite of nature-craving Vancouverites.

Just north of the parking lot, a wooden bridge provides access to Klineline Pond, where a short paved trail leads to a stocked fishing hole and more-developed areas like a kid-populated spray park and a roped-off swimming area. Back on the main trail, past a sports-field complex, Salmon Creek dashes in from the right along pebble-strewn banks and channels undergoing restoration efforts. By 0.5 mile, the urban park areas vanish and a large pond marks a popular waypoint. A reliable cast of western painted turtles are often seen basking in the sun. Continue around a curve and you'll see the wetlands sprawling out between walls of conifers guarding the perimeters. Reclusive critters like river otters, beavers, and muskrats reside in the marshy realm.

At 1.6 miles the path abruptly enters the forest, burrowing across a lush hillside. Here you'll encounter Cougar Creek, which tumbles out of a stand of brawny firs, excavating a gulley with curvaceous layers of dark rocks. The Cougar Creek Trail rises to the left, offering a 0.5-mile detour beside the creek. On the main path, the final 1.5 miles skirt just above the wetlands, allowing excellent bird-watching. Near the walk's end at NW 36th Avenue, the sight of Mount Hood's snowy crown to the south puts an exclamation point on a morning spent exploring this resilient urban refuge.

ADDRESS: 1112 NE 117th Street, Vancouver, WA

GETTING THERE: From I-5 N in Vancouver, take exit 7A for NE 134th and turn right. Go 0.1 mile and turn right onto NE 20th, which becomes Highway 99. Continue 0.7 mile and turn right onto NE 117 Street. Go 0.2 mile to the park entrance on the right.

CONTACT: Vancouver Parks and Recreation, (360) 397-2285, clark.wa.gov/public-works/salmon-creek-regional-parkklineline-pond

35 BURNT BRIDGE CREEK GREENWAY TRAIL– STEWART GLEN

Vancouver, WA, 14 miles north of downtown Portland

Tranquil lake waters, open fields, and dense forest line this suburban Vancouver path.

TRAIL	Up to 8 miles; 1.5 miles one way as described here
STEEPNESS	Gentle
OTHER USES	Bicycles
DOGS	On leash
CONNECTING TRAILS	Ellen Davis Trail
PARK AMENITIES	Restroom (available April 1 to October 31)
DISABLED ACCESS	Yes

An eastern backwater finger of Vancouver Lake forms the western head of Stewart Glen, a sylvan, 1.5-mile section of the 8-mile-long Burnt Bridge Creek Greenway Trail. The trailhead is lined with a lake overlook that's been clustered with plantings that attract native birds. A smooth blacktop path ushers walkers into a dewy forest with large firs, maples, alders, and ferns spilling down a steep slope. If you've forgotten your Fitbit, circular metal signs embedded in the path and painted mile markers appear every 0.25 miles, helping runners, dog walkers, birders, and other neighborhood users gauge steps. Among the triangulated awning of tree limbs, look for spotted towhees, robins, and wrens, while listening carefully for hawks crying *screeee* above.

After passing an impressive grove of western red cedars at 0.8 mile, the path leaves the forest and splits to border a large, sunny ellipse of purple-hued grassland by a power line. Tree swallows careen around the swaying blades, and red-tailed hawks and other raptors often stalk the sky above.

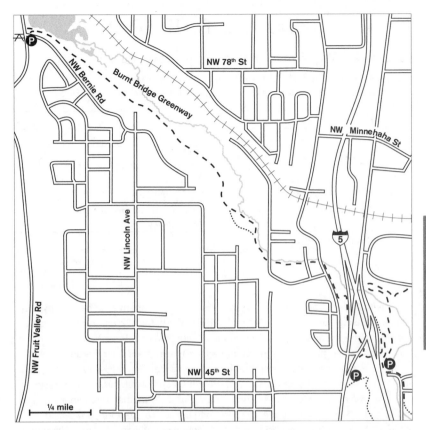

Gurgling little Burnt Bridge Creek makes an appearance after the paths rejoin, and at 1.3 miles a pretty bridge crossing on a bend might come with a color guard of mallards dawdling in a petite lawn nearby.

The path traces the creek from this point but concludes in 0.2 mile, after crossing two small roads and winding behind fenced-off pastures and houses to reach NE Hazel Dell Avenue. If you want to keep walking, head to the right, following a brown sign for the Burnt Bridge Creek Greenway Trail, and cross over I-5 on a pedestrian bridge to explore Leverich Park and beyond.

ADDRESS: NW Fruit Valley Road and NW Bernie Drive, Vancouver, WA

GETTING THERE: From I-5 N in Vancouver, take exit 4 and turn left onto NE 78th Street. Go 1.3 miles to NW Lake Shore and turn left. NW Lake Shore becomes Fruit Valley Road. Go 0.3 mile and turn left at NW Bernie Road. The trailhead is on the left. Park along NW Bernie Road.

CONTACT: Vancouver Parks and Recreation, (360) 487-8311, cityofvancouver.us/parksrec

<u>36</u> FRENCHMAN'S BAR TRAIL

Vancouver, WA, 16 miles north of downtown Portland

A smooth blacktop path connects two crown jewels of the
Vancouver park system, exploring river, lake, and forest habitats.

TRAIL	6 miles round-trip
STEEPNESS	Gentle
OTHER USES	Bicycles
DOGS	On leash
CONNECTING TRAILS	Vancouver Lake Trail, Vancouver Lake Regional Park
PARK AMENITIES	Restrooms, interpretive signs, sand volleyball courts, sports fields, picnic shelters
DISABLED ACCESS	Yes

The paved 3-mile Frenchman's Bar Trail, just east of Vancouver, is flanked by two equally pleasing (and distinct) Pacific Northwest settings: 120-acre Frenchman's Bar Regional Park and 234-acre Vancouver Lake Regional Park. You can start the outing from either park, and a midpoint trailhead even splits the difference.

For riverside exploration, begin at Frenchman's Bar Regional Park. About 0.5 mile of blacktop path traverse the park. From the south, walk through a grassy lawn and survey Mounts Saint Helens, Adams, and Hood, then ditch your kicks and stroll back along the beach for more than a mile. To the north, a 0.5-mile gravel path visits a cottonwood forest and a sandy beach accented with driftwood.

Known as the Columbia Lowlands, the surrounding floodplain habitat is an avian extravaganza for migratory birds. About fifty species of ducks and numerous other long-haul travelers, such as sandhill cranes and snow geese, pass through annually—a fact that's evident as you walk between the two parks. From Frenchman's Bar's north end, the paved trail follows along NW Lower River Road, bisecting two farms with clouds of birds flying overhead. In 1.5 miles, an alternate trailhead surveys Portland's Kelley Point Park (Walk #18) and the wide mouth of the Willamette River.

Follow the path along a channel, which empties into Vancouver Lake, and watch for red-winged blackbirds and cruising herons. Across NW Lower River Road, enter the 230-acre Vancouver Lake Regional Park. Windsurfing, kayaking, and

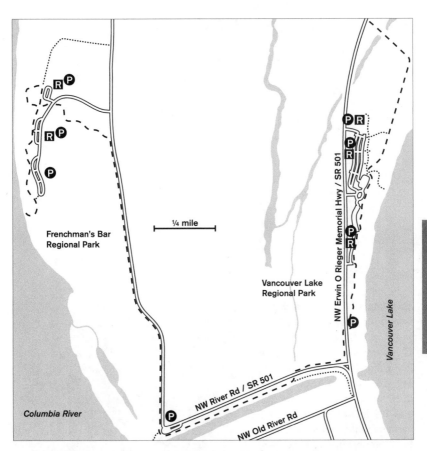

Frenchman's Bar
Regional Park

¼ mile

Vancouver Lake
Regional Park

NW Erwin O Rieger Memorial Hwy / SR 501

Vancouver Lake

Columbia River

NW River Rd / SR 501

NW Old River Rd

crew races all make for a busy aquatic scene. But the lake is also a good place to spot grebes, loons, and gulls.

Stroll by a developed beach area and a corridor of maples. A jewelweed-lined gravel lane then bends toward the quiet oak-lined Buckmire Slough. Look for the new 1-mile barrier-free path opened along this stretch in 2016. Hemmed in by a mature forest of cottonwoods and alders, the path doesn't offer lake views, but copious bird chatter engages eardrums, and a profusion of deciduous leaves keep the area primed for fall foliage viewing.

ADDRESS: 9612 NW Lower River Road, Vancouver, WA

GETTING THERE: From I-5 N, take exit 1D for Fourth Plain and go west. In 2 miles Fourth Plain turns into NW Lower River Road (WA 501). Continue 4.5 miles and look for the park entrance on the left.

CONTACT: Vancouver Parks and Recreation, (360) 397-2285, clark.wa.gov/public-works/frenchmans-bar-regional-park

37 COLUMBIA SPRINGS

Vancouver, WA, 17.5 miles northeast of downtown Portland

A trio of short loops at this urban nature center and historic fish hatchery add up to a great family destination.

TRAIL	2 miles
STEEPNESS	Gentle
OTHER USES	Students on field trips
DOGS	On leash
CONNECTING TRAILS	Evergreen Highway Trail
PARK AMENITIES	Restrooms, interpretive displays, educational programs
DISABLED ACCESS	None

The waters of Columbia Springs have been busy for nearly 200 years. In 1828 the Hudson's Bay Company erected the region's first water-powered sawmill here. Ten years later, the liquid turned giant stones in a three-story-tall gristmill. In 1938 WPA workers harnessed the water for the historic Vancouver Trout Hatchery, which is still in use. Today the springs, which dribble up from aquifers created by ancient Columbia River floodplain deposits, serve as the catalyst for the namesake 100-acre environmental educational center and natural area.

A myriad of bite-size habitats flourish here: deciduous woodlands, ponds, and a pair of wetland lakes. Located in an urban corner of Vancouver, just east of I-205, it's a haven for wood

ducks, deer, otters, beavers, Pacific tree frogs, rough-skinned newts, herons, egrets, and other animals. Three short paths dip into the preserve, providing an equally refreshing respite for city dwellers.

Accessed through ponds of the trout hatchery, the 1-mile Heron Loop leading to West and East Biddle Lakes is especially pleasing. Outfitted with tiered boardwalks, the loop skirts above the skunk cabbage–filled waters of West Biddle Lake, then offers a spur into a meadow dotted with small evergreens that leads to a quiet viewing platform above East Biddle Lake. Double back to the Heron Loop to traverse a shrub-lined pond filled with lilies and chatty ducks, and return to the hatchery.

At the west end of the parking lot, a chain of short trails is worth a quick jaunt. On the 0.3-mile Trillium Trail, wind through a verdant understory of Indian plum and snowberry. Then follow the paved Evergreen Highway Trail past a display of the old gristmill and toward the Glenn Jackson Bridge. Just beneath the overpass, the 0.5-mile Cedar Circle Trail darts into stands of maple and alder on a lollipop circuit, passing a bird blind and a rustic shelter.

ADDRESS: 12208 SE Evergreen Highway, Vancouver, WA

GETTING THERE: From I-205 N, take WA 14 E to the 164th Street exit. Turn right on Evergreen Highway and drive west to Columbia Springs.

CONTACT: Columbia Springs, (360) 882-0936, columbiasprings.org

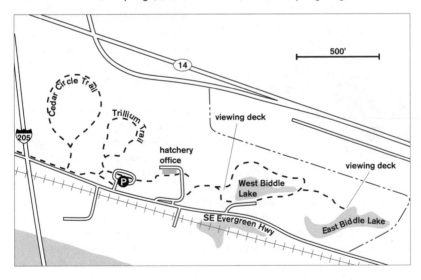

38 RIDGEFIELD NATIONAL WILDLIFE REFUGE OAKS TO WETLANDS TRAIL

Ridgefield, WA, 27 miles north of downtown Portland

Discover rich native culture and explore a timeless landscape of wetlands, woodlands, and forest lakes.

TRAIL	2-mile loop
STEEPNESS	Gentle
OTHER USES	Pedestrians only
DOGS	Not allowed
CONNECTING TRAILS	None
PARK AMENITIES	Restrooms, interpretive displays and structures, naturalist-led walks, volunteers
DISABLED ACCESS	Trail to Cathlapotle Plankhouse

Most Portlanders probably didn't feel the 1964 quake that shook the Copper River Delta in Alaska. But for one of our local avian residents, it had a profound effect. The dusky Canada goose, which winters exclusively in the lower Columbia River Valley, saw its summer nesting grounds along the Copper River drastically altered by the seismic upheaval. With their numbers in swift decline, wildlife officials acted to protect the geese's winter habitat in the Northwest by establishing Ridgefield National Wildlife Refuge in 1965.

In 2015 this 5,200-acre convergence of oak woodlands, wetlands, grasslands, and dense fir forests in western Clark County celebrated its fiftieth anniversary. Divided into five management units, only two of which are open to the public, the historic preserve now supports more than two hundred bird species, including herons, ducks, swans, warblers, swallows, and winter squadrons of the distinctive tuxedo-necked dusky Canada goose. Walks around the refuge's Carty Unit's easy 2-mile loop reveal that this refuge also safeguards significant cultural heritage.

From the refuge headquarters, cross a modernist curved bridge that opened in 2015, and enjoy a gaping view of Carty Lake and wooded Bachelor Island flanking the Columbia River. Down a gravel path, you'll encounter the Cathlapotle Plankhouse. Constructed in 2005 during the bicentennial of the Lewis and Clark expedition, this remarkable western red cedar structure along Gee Creek is a full-scale replica of the Chinook-built structures the explorers encountered here in 1805, a time when the area held the largest concentration of Native Americans in North America. (On spring and summer weekends, volunteers offer tours inside the plank-house, which are highly recommended.)

Ahead, pass a small stone plaza shaded by a 400-year-old Oregon white oak. As you enter the forest, tall firs and western red cedars block out the sky, while star-flowered Solomon's seals pop like tiny flashbulbs below. Approaching Boot Lake at the 0.7-mile mark, the trail gets brushy and overgrown. This northern area of the refuge extends onto private property, so heed occasional closure signs.

As the trail begins its loop back around to the south, look for a path to the right leading up to a series of "oak balds"—mounds of basalt outcroppings. Dotted with sun-singed grass, scrub oaks, and scores of flowers like camas, blue-eyed Mary,

and sea blush, these spots are an unforgettable perch where you can scan for coyotes, river otters, and the refuge's newest residents looking for a rebound, the recently reintroduced Columbian white-tailed deer.

ADDRESS: 28908 NW Main Avenue, Ridgefield, WA

GETTING THERE: From I-5 N in Vancouver, take exit 14 and drive west on WA 501 / Pioneer Street into the town of Ridgefield. Turn right on N Main Avenue and go 1 mile to the Carty Unit of the wildlife refuge, located on the left. There is a $3 entrance fee.

CONTACT: US Fish and Wildlife Service, Ridgefield National Wildlife Refuge, (360) 887-4106, fws.gov /refuge/ridgefield

<u>39</u> RIDGEFIELD NATIONAL WILDLIFE REFUGE KIWA TRAIL

Ridgefield, WA, 27 miles north of downtown Portland

An ADA-compliant path loops between sloughs, lakes, and an ash forest with a jaw-dropping amount of birds and plants.

TRAIL	1.5-mile loop
STEEPNESS	Gentle
OTHER USES	Pedestrians only
DOGS	Not allowed
CONNECTING TRAILS	None
PARK AMENITIES	None
DISABLED ACCESS	Yes

Open from May 1 through September 30, this fully accessible crushed-gravel path is located in the River S Unit of the Ridgefield National Wildlife Refuge, about 2 miles south of the Oaks to Wetlands Trail (Walk #38). Reaching the trailhead means cruising a portion of the refuge's popular auto tour route, which rambles down a one-way dirt road past a series of lakes filled with American bitterns, cinnamon teals, long-billed dowitchers, and egrets.

Of course, you came to walk. And the Kiwa Trail delivers. Winding between a cluster of four lakes that are edged by a forest of Oregon ash trees, the path begins over the still waters of the Bower Slough. Here you'll see western painted turtles lazing on fallen branches and Pacific tree frogs bounding toward the reeds. The furry crowns of muskrats and nutrias bob up like aquatic prairie dogs.

To the right, the trail wanders into an ash forest that attracts swallows, waxwings, grosbeaks, wrens, and woodpeckers. The acrobatic tree swallows are especially visible as the trail approaches the grass-filled South East Lake. Signs throughout the site remind visitors to be quiet: "*Shhhh* . . . Turtles Snoozing, Birds Resting." An extended

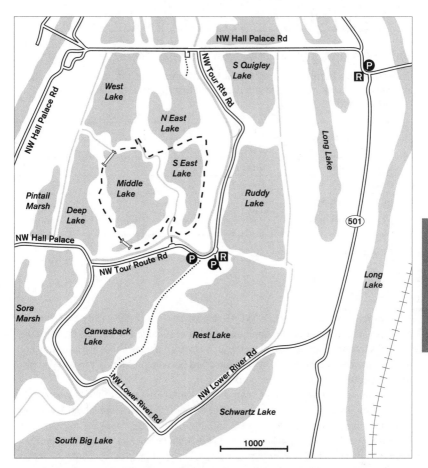

boardwalk provides passage over the northern end of Middle Lake. Curious nutrias will likely appear along this stretch. On the trail's southern stretches, look back to see the snowy dome of Mount Saint Helens looming above the green grasses.

ADDRESS: Refuge Road and S Hillhurst, Ridgefield, WA

GETTING THERE: From I-5 N in Vancouver, take exit 14 and drive west on WA 501 / Pioneer Street. At 9th Ave turn left and continue on S Hillhurst Road. Turn right at the River S Unit entrance and go downhill. Cross a one-lane bridge to an information kiosk and restrooms. Follow the auto tour route for 0.5 mile until you reach the signposted trailhead on the right. The trail is open May 1 to September 30, and there is a $3 entrance fee.

CONTACT: US Fish and Wildlife Service, Ridgefield National Wildlife Refuge, (360) 887-4106, fws.gov/refuge/ridgefield

<u>40</u> LEWISVILLE REGIONAL PARK

Battle Ground, WA, 28 miles northeast of downtown Portland

*Treasured by generations of Clark County residents, this
154-acre park delivers a scenic stroll along the Lewis River
and forested hillsides.*

TRAIL	2.5 miles
STEEPNESS	Gentle to moderate
OTHER USES	Bicycles
DOGS	On leash
CONNECTING TRAILS	None
PARK AMENITIES	Restrooms, group picnic shelters, boat launch, sports fields, tennis and basketball courts
DISABLED ACCESS	Yes

Considered the best large-scale WPA-era project in the county, 154-acre Lewisville Regional Park is listed on the National Register of Historic Places. Not that anyone here has forgotten about it. Visiting the park on a sunny day can feel like stumbling into Southwest Washington's largest backyard barbeque. But don't worry—you're invited, and there's lots of room to spread out.

Set along a gorgeous tree-covered bend of the East Fork of the Lewis River, the park perimeter is outlined by a roughly elliptical 3-mile natural-surface walking path. One main road bisects the park and the trail. The east side of the path fronts the river for more than a mile and passes the highly trafficked Central Commons area. The western half also stretches about a mile but rises up to a stealthy forested ridgeline that's usually visited only by dedicated walkers.

Walking along the eastern edge, you'll visit sprawling greens alive with every conceivable kind of lawn game and the sizzle of charcoal grills. The river also beckons along this section. There are sandy swimming beaches and boulder-rimmed perches to scope the flowing waters. And while some trails might have cairns to mark the way, here you'll gauge your whereabouts by a handsome collection of WPA-built picnic shelters. Thirteen of these log-hewn structures dot the path and look akin to national park lodges, with exposed beams and oversize stonework fireplaces.

On the west side, the path undulates along a quiet hillside. Robins hopscotching through the brush and spotted towhees peering down from alder branches provide company here and will likely add to the many lasting impressions of this classic Northwest park.

ADDRESS: 26411 NE Lewisville Highway, Battle Ground, WA

GETTING THERE: From I-5 N, take exit 11 and turn east on NE 219th Street / WA 502. Go 6 miles and turn left on NW 10th Avenue / WA 503. Go 2 miles and look for the park entrance on the right. Continue on the Park Drive for 0.7 mile and look for the trailhead by the Hemlock Shelter, behind the baseball field.

CONTACT: Vancouver Parks and Recreation, (360) 397-2285, clark.wa.gov/public-works/lewisville -regional-park

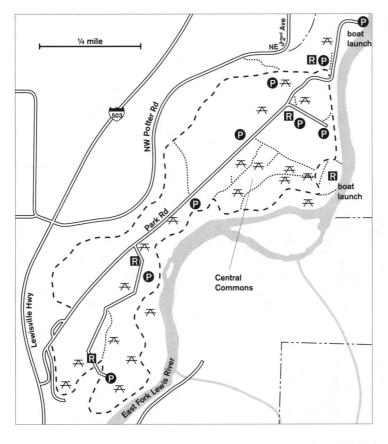

41 BATTLE GROUND LAKE STATE PARK

Battle Ground, WA, 29 miles north of downtown Portland

Ring a 2-mile path around a volcanic crater lake and then plunge into the refreshing waters.

TRAIL	Up to 10 miles; 2 miles as described here
STEEPNESS	Gentle to moderate
OTHER USES	Bicycle and horse trails intersect with designated pedestrian trails
DOGS	On leash
CONNECTING TRAILS	None
PARK AMENITIES	Restrooms, picnic shelters, overnight camping, boat launch, swimming
DISABLED ACCESS	None

Volcanically speaking, Battle Ground Lake State Park hasn't been active for at least 100,000 years. But on hot days, the 28-acre lake surface, which formed eons ago when rising superhot magma encountered chilly subterranean water, springs to life in the form of swarms of Washingtonians drawn to its timbered oasis.

From the parking lot, follow the paved route straight down to the shore. A roped-off swimming beach on the right will likely be in full swing. To circumnavigate the waters, head left, near a dock, into the cooling forest where the Lower Lake Trail wedges between a steep slope and the lake water. Numerous fallen

logs poke into the water like woodsy diving boards. Almost any spot is good for a quick dip or extended sunbathing. Motorboats are not allowed. Instead you'll observe human-oared crafts quietly gliding along the surface. Rounding the lake, basalt grottos rise overhead, dainty flowers line the ground, and stellar jays dart furtively among the trees.

Just short of the 1-mile mark, you can leave the lake scene behind and track the Upper Lake Trail. This wide, gently rising path ascends into the forest, where thick tree limbs muffle the sound of splashing while still allowing occasional watery overlooks. Continue past walk-in campsites hidden in the woods and a pair of lonely trailside benches, seemingly long forgotten.

At 1.2 miles look to the right for a faint side trail up to the Marshall Overlook, where you'll find a memorial stone bench in a screen of pines. High above the lake, the overlook is the perfect place for a dose of solitude. Heading back down, look for a T intersection and turn left to return to the dock.

ADDRESS: 18002 NE 249th Street, Battle Ground, WA

GETTING THERE: From I-5 N in Vancouver, take exit 11 and follow WA 502 for 6 miles to Battle Ground. Continue east on Main Street and turn left onto NE Grace Avenue, which becomes NE 142nd Avenue. Go 0.5 mile and turn right onto NE 10th, which becomes NE Heisson Road. Go 1.4 miles and head right on NE 244th Street. Go 1 mile and turn left into the park. A Discover Pass or a $10 day pass is required.

CONTACT: Washington State Parks, (360) 687-4621, parks.state.wa.us

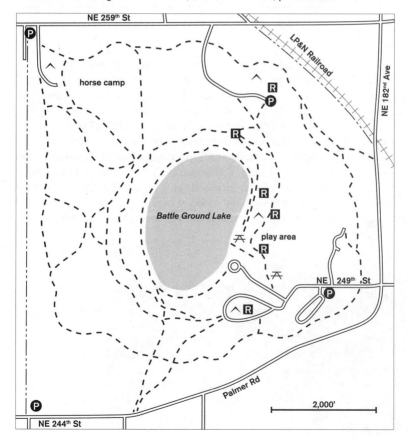

42 LA CENTER BOTTOMS

La Center, WA, 27 miles north of Portland

Walk along a restored floodplain habitat at this Watchable Wildlife site in Clark County.

TRAIL	2 miles
STEEPNESS	Gentle
OTHER USES	Horses
DOGS	On leash
CONNECTING TRAILS	None
PARK AMENITIES	Restrooms at Sternwheeler Park, interpretive signs, bird blinds
DISABLED ACCESS	Yes

Situated along 3,500 feet of the East Fork of the Lewis River shoreline, the La Center Bottoms trail wraps through a wide floodplain laced with creeks, seasonal lakes, ponds, upland forest, and lazy river currents. In fall and winter it's a layover for migrating tundra swan and Canada geese. Permanent denizens include northern harriers, barn swallows, river otters, black-tailed deer, and coyotes. This diverse menagerie earned the location a state designation as a Watchable Wildlife site.

A $2 million restoration effort spearheaded by the Bonneville Power Administration and the Lower Columbia Estuary Partnership in 2015 aims to make La Center Bottoms even better. More than sixty thousand native trees and shrubs were planted in the hopes of shading out some of the prevalent invasive grasses—much of which sprang up from past cattle grazing operations. The old levee that forms the walking

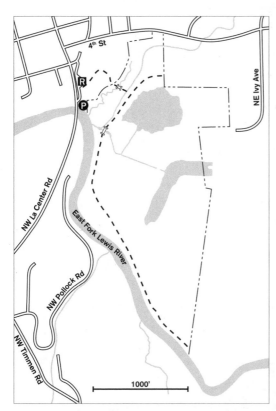

route has been strategically breached with meandering channels that reconnect the bottomlands to the East Fork's historic floodplain and provide curves that act like rest stops for migrating chum and Coho salmon.

Within a few steps of the trailhead you can also visit adjoining Sternwheeler Park. A sculpture-lined gazebo and amphitheater make this an attractive spot to inspect interpretive displays noting La Center's (so named because of its central location between early pioneer settlements) heyday as a sternwheeler port of commerce.

Wetland explorations start across a small bridge over Brezee Creek. Turn right at the junction onto a wide dirt-and-gravel path. A pair of bird blinds invites you to gaze over conical tufts of hardhack flowers in search of herons, geese, and mallards stationed among pads of skunk cabbage. The gravel trail ends after 0.5 mile at a small footbridge. A grassy double-track path takes over, continuing another 0.5 mile before ending at the corner of a large pasture. Along this stretch, the path borders the slow-moving East Fork of the Lewis River. Bedded-down grasses hint at recent deer activity. On the opposite bank, look for red-tailed hawks and harriers rotating above layers of cottonwoods and western hemlocks.

ADDRESS: 101 Aspen Avenue, La Center, WA

GETTING THERE: From I-5 N in Vancouver, take exit 16 and turn right onto La Center Road. Go 1.7 miles. Take the first right after crossing the bridge, and look for the park entrance on the right, behind the water reclamation plant.

CONTACT: Clark County Parks, (360) 397-2285, clark.wa.gov/parks

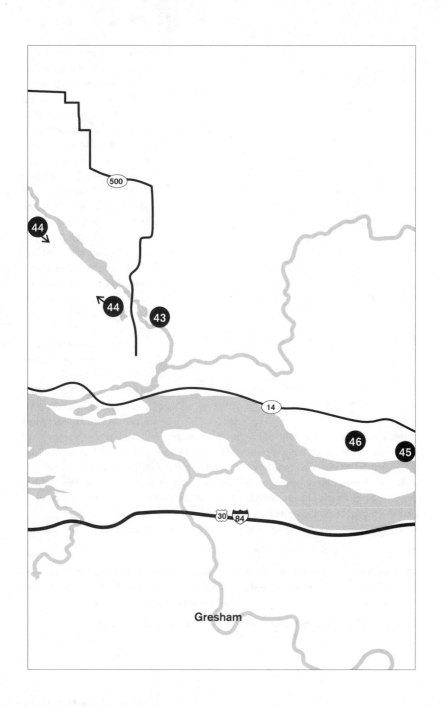

SOUTHWEST WASHINGTON

<u>43</u> LACAMAS LAKE REGIONAL PARK

Camas, WA, 14 miles northeast of downtown Portland

A lake, a trio of waterfalls, and meadows of camas highlight this 312-acre treasure.

TRAIL	Up to 6 miles; 2.5-mile loop as described here
STEEPNESS	Gentle to moderate
OTHER USES	Bicycles
DOGS	On leash
CONNECTING TRAILS	Lacamas Heritage Trail (Walk #44), Washougal River Greenway Trail
PARK AMENITIES	Restrooms, interpretive displays, playground
DISABLED ACCESS	None

Donated to Clark County by the Crown Zellerbach paper company in 1964, Lacamas Lake Regional Park has blossomed into a gift for the entire Metro area and should be on any Portlander's to-walk list. Within its 312 acres you'll find a rushing stream, shimmery waterfalls, fields of wildflowers, and a tree-ringed lake to boot. The park's 6 miles of web trails allow numerous loop options.

The developed picnic area fronting Round Lake, which forms the northeast corner of the park, makes a good home base, with several park maps and kiosks covering the history of the watershed. For a mellow outing, try the 1.2-mile interpretive path around the lake and inspect a pair of dams at the southern end. Installed in 1883 (and updated in the 1930s to power mill operations in Camas), the structures raised the lake water 12 feet. Traverse the spillway to see a deluge

of white water crash into Lacamas Creek below. Across the dam, a short side trail to the right leads to a view of the Potholes, a waterfall so named because of the depressions in the eroded soft rock around it. Continue southward along the creek from the Potholes to reach the scenic Lower Falls, which tumble over a wide staircase of rocks beneath a photogenic footbridge.

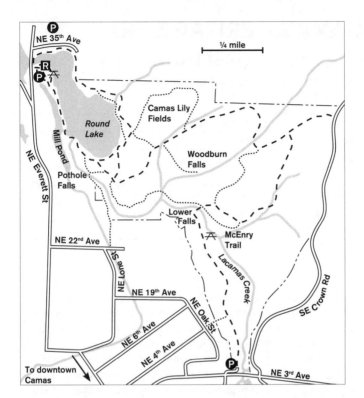

In springtime, it's all about the camas flowers. From the dam, follow the well-signposted Camas Lily Loop for 0.2 mile to the base of a forested mound. Keep right at a Y junction by a park signpost, and head left up a trail marked by a blue "Natural Area" sign. Ascend a series of terraced stone outcrops that divvy up pocket meadows swimming with pointy camas flowers and lanky grasses. Atop the bluff you can drop down the opposite side to rejoin the Round Lake Loop.

Back at the Y junction for the Camas Lily Loop, a wooden post points the way to Woodburn Falls. Best viewed in the spring, during high creek levels, this cascade drops 20 feet, forming a lacy sheet over a wall of dark basalt at the crux of a secluded ravine.

ADDRESS: 3344 NE Everett Street, Camas, WA

GETTING THERE: From I-205 N, take WA 14 (Lewis and Clark Highway) to exit 12 for downtown Camas. Follow signs for WA 14 and look for a junction with WA 500 N (passing a junction with WA 500 S). Turn left (north) onto WA 500, which becomes NE Everett Street. Follow NE Everett just past NW Lake Road, and look for the park on the right.

CONTACT: Clark County Parks, (360) 397-2285, clark.wa.gov/parks

44 LACAMAS HERITAGE TRAIL

Camas, WA, 14 miles northeast of downtown Portland

Walk a lakeshore for 3 miles among large trees and a secluded wetland.

TRAIL	3.5 miles one way
STEEPNESS	Gentle
OTHER USES	Bicycles
DOGS	On leash
CONNECTING TRAILS	Lacamas Lake Regional Park (Walk #43)
PARK AMENITIES	Restrooms, interpretive displays
DISABLED ACCESS	Yes

Legend has it that while rowing a boat across Lacamas Lake, Henry Pittock, the larger-than-life owner of the *Oregonian*, leaned over the water and declared this area would make a great place to build a paper mill. In 1883, that's just what he did, establishing the town of LaCamas (later shortened to Camas, after the blue lily common here) with the construction of a large mill a few miles to the east. More than 130 years later, Camas still boasts a mill-town heritage, and Lacamas Lake remains an inspiration for those who gaze upon its waters—although you're likely to aspire to something a bit humbler than empire building. Namely, a lovely walk.

Extending the length of the lake, this 3.5-mile mostly flat graveled path pro-

vides a meditative stroll down a largely undeveloped shoreline. Placid waters abound. As do pebbly, log-scattered coves for rock tossing. There are titanic trees to ogle and wetlands for birding. Flowering thimbleberries, Pacific bleeding heart, and trillium add to the color palette.

Departing Heritage Park, at the lake's southeastern edge, travel westward, leaving the grassy lawn, on a paved path along NW Lake Road to join a crushed-gravel trail tucked against the lake. Pass among large western red cedars and arching alder branches to reach a boat ramp at 1.4 miles.

Just up from the boat ramp, the trail keeps right and out of view of the lake on a narrow

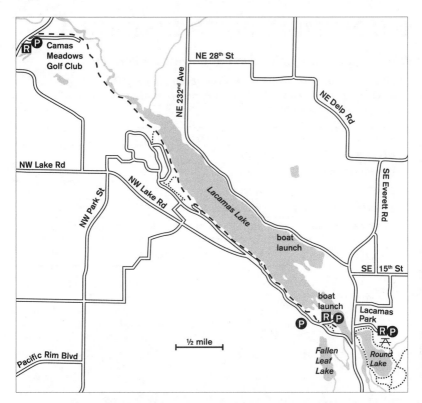

green field set beneath stately homes rising above. Soon the trail meets the lake again, passing a few large waterfront houses and private docks. Around 2 miles, the lake transitions into a wetland slough sprouting alders, red osier dogwoods, and cattails. A trio of handsome bridges forms ideal clearings for spotting red-winged blackbirds, kingfishers, wood ducks, eagles, and ospreys.

Beyond the last bridge, the trail meets a power-line corridor, marking a good turnaround point. For those determined to finish the course (or just in need of a bathroom), continue 0.5 mile ahead, skirting by the Camas Meadows Golf Club, to an alternate trailhead at NE Goodwin Road with restrooms and water fountains.

ADDRESS: 227 NW Lake Road, Camas, WA

GETTING THERE: From I-205 N, take WA 14 (Lewis and Clark Highway) to exit 12 for downtown Camas. Follow signs for WA 14 and look for a junction with WA 500 N (passing a junction with WA 500 S). Turn left (north) onto WA 500, which becomes NE Everett Street. Follow NE Everett Street, turn left on NW Lake Road, and look for the park entrance on the right.

CONTACT: Clark County Parks, (360) 397-2285, clark.wa.gov/parks

<u>45</u> COLUMBIA RIVER DIKE TRAIL

Washougal, WA, 23 miles east of downtown Portland

Stroll atop a floating walkway at Steamboat Landing Park, then explore a historic Lewis and Clark encampment at the edge of a bird-rich wildlife refuge.

TRAIL	4 miles one way
STEEPNESS	Gentle
OTHER USES	Bicycles, horses
DOGS	On leash
CONNECTING TRAILS	Gibbons Creek Wildlife Art Trail (Walk #46)
PARK AMENITIES	Restrooms, interpretive displays, pavilions, picnic shelters
DISABLED ACCESS	Yes

This path on top of a levee in Washougal stretches for 3 miles along the Columbia River, moving walkers between a pair of riverside parks, a famous Lewis and Clark canoe landing and encampment, and the 1,049-acre Steigerwald Lake National Wildlife Refuge.

Connected to downtown Washougal via a pedestrian tunnel beneath WA 14, Steamboat Landing Park, at the west end of the route, marks a popular starting point. A floating walkway puts you right on the river, where fisherman cast lines for leaping bass and steelhead against the craggy backdrop of Mount Hood. Uphill from

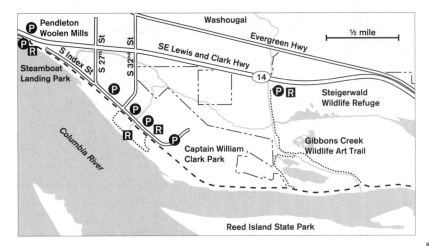

the walkway, the dike trail is as flat as a ruler, with a thick line of cottonwoods providing the only break in the Columbia River shoreline to the right. (An industrial section of Washougal lays to the left but does little to distract from the magnetic appeal of the river.)

Just shy of a mile, edge into Captain William Clark Park, where tall cottonwoods swirl with ospreys. (A large osprey nest can be spotted atop a pole in the corner of the lumberyard to the left.) The park's timber-framed Recognition Plaza marks a path to Cottonwood Beach, where wide picnic lawns and riverfront coves occupy a significant Corps of Discovery footprint. Lewis and Clark's 6-day stint here during their return was their longest encampment along this section of the Columbia River, and the visit provided Captain Clark, along with his Native American guides, an opportunity to chart the Willamette River, a point they had initially missed on their westward trek.

Past Cottonwood Beach, the dike enters Steigerwald Lake National Wildlife Refuge. The setting grows more rural as you pass an open field with a dilapidated barn. To the right look for bubble-like birdhouses placed to aid purple martins. At 3 miles, pass a link with the Gibbons Creek Wildlife Art Trail (Walk #46). At 3.5 miles, by a second trail entrance to Gibbons Creek, an overlook above a fish ladder connecting to Gibbons Creek offers a spellbinding view of Mount Hood and Crown Point. The trail continues for another 0.5 mile to a fence line, though most locals choose this scenery-soaked spot as their turnaround point.

ADDRESS: 100 S Washougal River Road, Washougal, WA

GETTING THERE: From Vancouver, drive 16 miles east on WA 14 into Washougal. Turn right onto 15th Street into Steamboat Landing Park.

CONTACT: Washougal Parks, (360) 835-2662, cityofwashougal.us/parks

46 GIBBONS CREEK WILDLIFE ART TRAIL

Washougal, WA, 25 miles northeast of downtown Portland

Nature-themed art installations accentuate a plethora of wildlife sightings on this unique Columbia River Gorge National Scenic Area path.

TRAIL	2.75 miles
STEEPNESS	Gentle
OTHER USES	Pedestrians only
DOGS	Not allowed
CONNECTING TRAILS	Columbia River Dike Trail (Walk #45)
PARK AMENITIES	Restrooms, interpretive displays, art installations, naturalist-led walks
DISABLED ACCESS	Yes

The wildlife-sighting board hanging at the Gibbons Creek trailhead could inspire a naturalist version of "The Twelve Days of Christmas": *Twelve deer a runnin' . . . six geese a honkin' . . . two fleeing foxes, and an osprey in a cottonwood tree.* Granted, your own artistic reactions to critters in this mix of fields, streams, wetlands, cottonwoods, and oaks may differ (probably for the better). But that's exactly the point of this unique outing within the 1,049-acre Steigerwald Lake National Wildlife Refuge.

Opened in 2009, the trail sits just inside the Columbia River Gorge National Scenic Area and is one of only two wildlife art trails in the National Wildlife Refuge System. Commissioned works riffing on local flora and fauna dot the 2.75-mile path, aiming to engage, educate, and inspire visitors.

Natural muses include Mount Hood, which sits prominently across the Columbia River, and reeds waving above wide creeks and shallow lakes. For a bird, it is an ideal passageway between the Cascades, making this a hot zone for avian traffic. In fact, two hundred of the three hundred bird species in Clark County have been spotted here. All the more reason

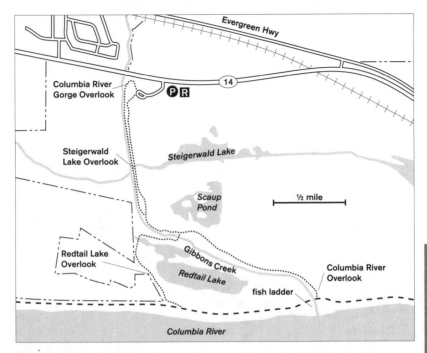

you might spot clouds of tundra swans or a solitary northern harrier clutching a garter snake in its claws.

At 0.5 mile a footbridge stands near a patch of cottonwoods and sun-bleached snags. A spur trail to the left is marked by an arched iron doorway that's both artistic and functional: if the door's open (this trail is closed from October 1 through April 30 to protect wintering waterfowl), step through for a 0.5-mile link to the Columbia River Dike Trail (Walk #45). At the junction with the dike trail take in a view of Crown Point, visible across the river, and walk 0.5 mile up the dike to access the southern end of the Gibbons Creek Wildlife Art Trail by Redtail Lake.

If the gate's closed for the season, head across the bridge, through an aisle of cottonwoods, to reach a long footbridge over Redtail Lake, a favorite hangout of western painted turtles and blue herons. You can link to the Columbia River Dike Trail straight ahead or return to the trailhead.

ADDRESS: 35001 Lewis and Clark Highway (WA 14), Washougal, WA

GETTING THERE: From I-205 in Vancouver, drive east on WA 14 for 18 miles and look for the trailhead on the right, just past a sign for the Columbia River Gorge National Scenic Area.

CONTACT: US Fish and Wildlife Service, Steigerwald Lake National Wildlife Refuge, (360) 835-8767, fws.gov/refuge/steigerwald_lake

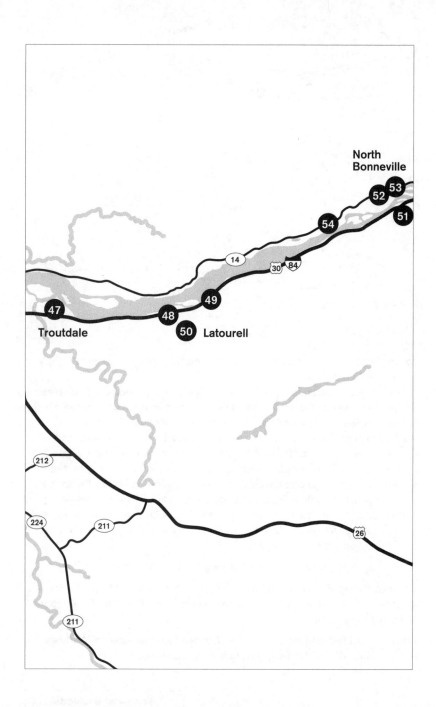

COLUMBIA RIVER GORGE

47 SANDY RIVER DELTA

Troutdale, OR, 25 miles east of downtown Portland

This 1,400-acre off-leash dog paradise is a doggone good place to go for a walk.

TRAIL	1.3 miles
STEEPNESS	Gentle
OTHER USES	Bicycles, horses
DOGS	Off leash except on the Confluence Trail
CONNECTING TRAILS	None
PARK AMENITIES	Restrooms
DISABLED ACCESS	Confluence Trail

When Lewis and Clark set foot along the Sandy River's muddy floodplain forests in 1805 (and again on their return in 1806), they were struck by the sheer numbers of birds and wildlife present. Today, it's the dogs that would go down in their journals.

Widely known as Thousand Acres, the delta (which actually measures 1,400 acres) has become Portland's de facto dog park. Every breed imaginable, from bushy-tailed Great Pyrenees to diminutive pugs, roams along a maze of trails that crisscross this former cattle pasture lodged between the Columbia River and I-84. And much of the park is designated as an off-leash area. So if you're averse to tail-wagging company, consider other options.

Aside from being a pooch nirvana, the delta sits inside the Columbia River Gorge National Scenic Area and ranks as one of the largest undeveloped Columbia River floodplain tracts within the Portland metro area. Native species like beavers, great blue herons, and northern red-legged frogs still have a toehold here. And long-term restoration efforts have been underway since the US Forest Service took ownership of the property in the 1990s. Most recently a small dam was removed in 2013, unclogging a channel between the Sandy and Columbia Rivers for the first time since the 1930s.

One can't-miss option: the 1.3-mile Confluence Trail—the only trail that requires pets to be on leash—tours the center of the park, providing Mount Hood views, on a track to the captivating Maya Lin–designed bird blind. Accessed from the graceful curve of a 150-foot-long boardwalk, the blind sits amid a 17-acre restoration area where willows and wetland flowers now gain ground on invasive reed canary grass. As part of the ambitious Confluence Project, which reinterprets key Lewis and Clark expedition sites from the perspective of Native Americans, this installation consists of vertical wood slats of sustainably sourced black locust. Each beam is inscribed with the name of an indigenous species, along with its current conservation status.

As many of the species are extinct or in peril, the bird blind is a sobering monument. Persistent bird chatter and the surrounding restorative efforts also make it a hopeful place that imparts a renewed vision for the delta.

ADDRESS: I-84 exit 18, Thousand Acres Road, Troutdale, OR

GETTING THERE: From I-84 E in Troutdale, take exit 18. Follow the loop beneath the highway and look for the signs for the Sandy River Delta on the left.

CONTACT: US Forest Service, (541) 308-1700, fs.usda.gov/crgnsa

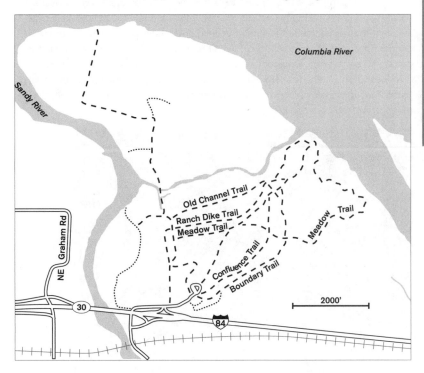

<u>48</u> ROOSTER ROCK STATE PARK

Corbett, OR, 23 miles east of downtown Portland

Take in river and distant waterfall views on a rolling ridge set in Rooster Rock State Park.

TRAIL	3-mile loop
STEEPNESS	Gentle to moderate
OTHER USES	Pedestrians only
DOGS	On leash
CONNECTING TRAILS	None
PARK AMENITIES	Restrooms, park visitor office, boat access, disc-golf course, picnic area
DISABLED ACCESS	None

The eye-catching pinnacle of Rooster Rock is the result of an ancient landslide emanating from the famous Crown Point viewpoint in the Columbia River Gorge, an event that somehow left this spire with an undeniably phallic look. And considering it now rises above a state park with the only designated nude beach in the gorge, it's as good an argument as any that the universe has a sense of humor. But junior high jokes aside, Rooster Rock State Park holds great trails for walking, particularly for those in search of uncrowded paths and great views absent the tough climbs so common in the gorge.

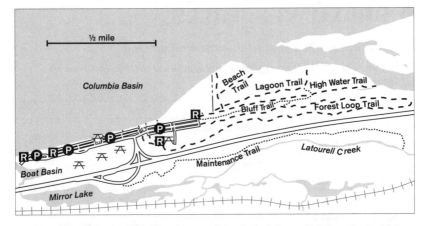

From a broad grassy lawn at the eastern edge of the park, follow the trail into a sliver of cottonwood trees, maples, and alders. Head right at the marked junction near a disc-golf course, into a rolling terrain that meanders up a ridgeline between the Columbia River and I-84 (the highway stays mainly shielded by a thick buffer of trees). Beneath the heavy canopy, the trail sports a spongy moss coating as it dips and rises. Cattails line the path, giving a hybrid wetland feel.

In spring you can expect a profusion of trillium blooms rising from seemingly every available patch of dirt. Around the 1-mile mark, the trail begins to slither around a fern-covered mound leading to a view of a low meadow and I-84 stretching to the east.

As the trail begins its loop back west, paralleling the highway, scan along the gorge walls for a series of falls tumbling down. A spectacular view of Crown Point rising across the highway also appears at 2.5 miles, as the trails dips into a bottomland and exits into a picnic area at the edge of the eastern parking area.

And what about the infamous rock? It's visible from the westernmost parking lot, above the boat-launch area.

ADDRESS: I-84 E at exit 25, Corbett, OR

GETTING THERE: From I-84 E, take exit 25, look for the park entrance, and turn right to reach the westernmost parking lot.

CONTACT: Oregon State Parks, (503) 695-2261, oregonstateparks.org

<u>49</u> BRIDAL VEIL FALLS

Bridal Veil, 28 miles east of downtown Portland

Easy-to-reach falls offer a quick jaunt, and a circular loop takes in historic highway views.

TRAIL	1.2 miles
STEEPNESS	Gentle to moderate
OTHER USES	Pedestrians only
DOGS	On leash
CONNECTING TRAILS	None
PARK AMENITIES	Restrooms, interpretive displays
DISABLED ACCESS	0.5-mile interpretive loop

One of the easiest Columbia River Gorge waterfalls to access, Bridal Veil Falls is a great complement to a longer day hike or is a good stand-alone leg-stretcher when a slower pace is desired. A bonus self-guided interpretive loop also provides outstanding viewpoints and an intriguing bit of history.

The falls portion starts on a paved track through the forest that quickly turns to gravel as it descends into a small canyon. Mossy stones line the path, leading to a petite footbridge and then a long set of stairs. With each step the roar of the falls grows louder. Once down the steps, you'll come to a bridge across Bridal Veil Creek, once the site of a thriving logging operation.

Across the footbridge, a small set of earthen stairs ascends to a viewing platform just a pebble's toss from the 120-foot cascade, which slides down from Larch Mountain in a frothy wedge broken up by a pair of rocky chutes. A trio of well-placed benches helps flagging walkers catch their breaths on the climb back out of the canyon.

Once back at the trailhead, head for the 0.5-mile paved loop starting near the restrooms. Along this level path, you'll encounter meadows filled with camas and a supporting cast of bead lily, trillium, and Pacific bleeding heart. A series of panoramic overlooks gazes over I-84, tracing the Columbia River, and features transportation-themed interpretive displays.

To the west, scan the tree line for the Pillars of Hercules. In the 1880s trains famously scraped between these imposing rock columns, with just inches to spare. But progress was inevitable. In the 1900s the track was rerouted to its current position north of the pillars to accommodate larger payloads. Today the rocks sit all but forgotten, slowly being swallowed by the forest.

ADDRESS: Historic Columbia River Highway Milepost 28, Bridal Veil, OR

GETTING THERE: From I-84 E, take exit 28. Go 0.4 mile and turn right (west) onto the Historic Columbia River Highway. Continue 0.7 mile to Bridal Veil Falls State Park.

CONTACT: Oregon State Parks, (503) 695-2261, oregonstateparks.org

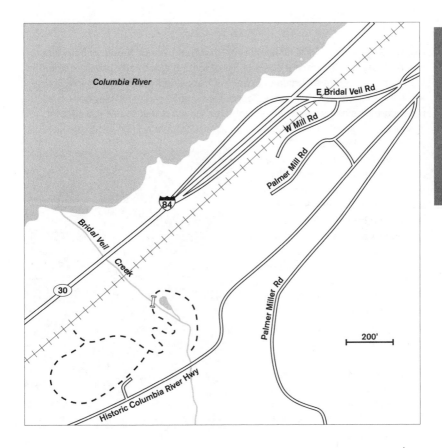

50 LATOURELL FALLS

Troutdale, 30 miles east of downtown Portland

A pair of showstopping waterfalls is accessible from a forested walk and a paved path.

TRAIL	2.3 miles
STEEPNESS	Moderate
OTHER USES	Pedestrians only
DOGS	On leash
CONNECTING TRAILS	None
PARK AMENITIES	Restrooms, interpretive displays
DISABLED ACCESS	Paved path to lower falls

Even in a crowded field of Columbia River Gorge gushers, Latourell Falls stands out. At 250 feet, this dazzler appears like a white braided rope dropped from the leafy heavens before a curtain of basalt rock speckled with moss. Visible just a few paces from the trailhead, Latourell also comes with a smaller but equally pleasing twin stashed in the canyon above. The short trek to see the second cascade, along with a link to a lower viewpoint of Latourell Falls, makes for a storybook-caliber walk.

A short paved climb from the road leads to the Latourell Falls upper viewing area. From here a rocky tread curves up above the falls among pillars of Douglas fir. The path soon levels out and traces Latourell Creek along a narrowing ravine filled with western red cedars. At 0.5 mile continue over a series of small bridges to reach a view of the upper falls, which plummet 120 feet into a splash pool at the crux of a misty canyon.

For the trek back, cross to the opposite side of Latourell Creek and head down amid thick patches of salals, sword ferns, and salmonberries. At 1.3 miles a sign for the loop

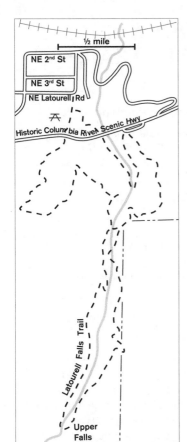

½ mile

NE 2ⁿᵈ St

NE 3ʳᵈ St

NE Latourell Rd

Historic Columbia River Scenic Hwy

Latourell Falls Trail

Upper Falls

trail leads up to the left, along a slope scattered with fragrant wildflowers. An overlook soon appears with mesmerizing sightlines to the Washington side of the gorge.

The trail now switchbacks down to meet the Historic Columbia River Highway. Cross the road, and follow the path down a set of stone stairs to a picnic area inside Guy W. Talbot State Park. Take the paved path to the right and wind beneath the cathedral-like arches of the historic highway underpass. Just ahead you'll reach the lower Latourell Falls area, where a mist-coated bridge provides a final look at the cascade shimmering down the canyon. A short paved path leads back out to the trailhead.

ADDRESS: Historic Columbia River Highway, 12 miles east of Troutdale, OR

GETTING THERE: From I-84 E, take exit 28, drive 0.4 mile, and turn right (west) onto the Historic Columbia River Highway. Continue 2.6 miles to the trailhead.

CONTACT: Oregon State Parks, (503) 695-2261, oregonstateparks.org

51 HISTORIC COLUMBIA RIVER HIGHWAY STATE TRAIL– TOOTH ROCK

Cascade Locks, 40 miles east of downtown Portland

The car-free Historic Columbia River Highway State Trail comes with views of the Columbia River and the Bonneville Lock and Dam.

TRAIL	2 miles
STEEPNESS	Gentle to moderate
OTHER USES	Bicycles
DOGS	On leash
CONNECTING TRAILS	Gorge Trail #400, Tanner Creek Trail, Wahclella Falls Trail
PARK AMENITIES	Interpretive signs; restrooms at Bonneville Lock and Dam and Eagle Creek
DISABLED ACCESS	Yes

Officially dedicated in 1916, the Historic Columbia River Highway was famously known as the King of Roads thanks to its landscape-hugging curves that allowed drivers to soak up the natural splendor of the Columbia River Gorge. A century later, it's walkers and bikers who sing the road's praises along the Historic Columbia River Highway State Trail, which repurposes bypassed segments of the old road as hiker-biker paths.

The Tooth Rock Trailhead near Bonneville Lock and Dam provides a great introduction to historic-highway walking with a 2-mile loop to a viaduct dating to 1915 that hangs over a cliff and does a return jaunt on a former wagon trail. You can also strike out on a 3.5-mile (one way) jaunt to Cascade Locks, where the car-free trail segment ends at the base of the Bridge of the Gods.

To reach the viaduct, follow the state highway trail eastward. You'll parallel I-84 for a short distance, then rise to the viaduct at 0.6 mile. An engineering marvel, this bridge-like ledge once allowed Model Ts to weave around the bulging basalt cliff face here (instead of barreling underneath it as I-84 does today). From this high perch, take in Beacon Rock, Bonneville Lock and Dam, Table Mountain, and possibly the sight of the Columbia Gorge Sternwheeler tour boat chugging along the river.

The trail then drops into a wooded pocket that stops at a set of stairs leading down to the Eagle Creek Trailhead, the Eagle Creek National Fish Hatchery

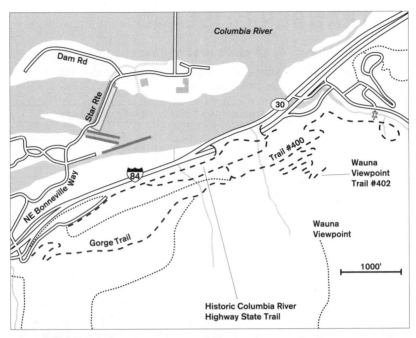

(0.2 mile away), and the next link in the state highway trail to Cascade Locks.

Just to the right of the stairway, an unpaved path climbs into the forest, providing an alternate return route through little-visited stands of Douglas fir. From the Toothrock Trailhead, you can also head west on the state highway trail to the John B. Yeon State Scenic Corridor (approximately 2 miles one way), which includes a crossing on the recently installed McCord Creek Bridge.

ADDRESS: I-84 exit 40, Bonneville Lock and Dam, Cascade Locks, OR

GETTING THERE: From I-84 E, take exit 40 for the Bonneville Lock and Dam, follow the road as it bends past the Wahclella Falls Trailhead entrance, and continue uphill 0.4 mile to reach the Tooth Rock Trailhead.

CONTACT: Oregon State Parks, (503) 695-2261, oregonstateparks.org

52 STRAWBERRY ISLAND

North Bonneville, WA, 48 miles east of downtown Portland

Find solitude and panoramic Columbia River Gorge views on this little-known outing in North Bonneville.

TRAIL	Approximately 3 miles; 2.1 miles as described here
STEEPNESS	Gentle
OTHER USES	Pedestrians only
DOGS	On leash
CONNECTING TRAILS	North Bonneville Heritage Trails
PARK AMENITIES	None
DISABLED ACCESS	None

Strawberry Island is more of a thick peninsula than an island, bulging into the Columbia River on the Washington side of the Columbia River Gorge. Noted as a stop on the Southwest Loop of the Washington Birding Trail, this 45-acre parcel is an exceptional place to see bald eagles, ospreys, and condor-size turkey vultures. Tucked away in tiny North Bonneville, Strawberry Island is also a great retreat from crowded gorge trails.

The island's striking topography consists of an open grassland that's book-

ended by a large treeless knoll to the east and a mixed-forested wetland on its western tip. An approximately 3-mile loop trail rounds the island, and walks come with the dazzling sensation of being surrounded by the towering forested walls of the gorge.

Along the island's cottonwood-lined western tip (about 0.75 miles from the main trailhead), a pair of viewpoints peeks out toward Hamilton Mountain and Beacon Rock, the famous landmark where Lewis and Clark first observed the tidal influence of the Pacific Ocean on the Columbia River. Rounding through the central grassland, you'll likely see red-winged blackbirds, swallows, Bullock's orioles, and plenty of scampering rabbits.

Climb the barren windswept mound to the east (less than 0.5 mile from the trailhead), and you'll feel like you've been transported to the Scottish Highlands. A knee-weakening 360-degree panorama includes vistas of the spillways of the Bonneville Lock and Dam, Beacon Rock, Hamilton Mountain, and the primordial-looking silhouettes of blue herons and turkey vultures flapping amid the 1,500-foot cliff faces of the gorge.

ADDRESS: Portage Drive, North Bonneville, WA

GETTING THERE: From I-84 E, take exit 44 at Cascade Locks and cross the Bridge of the Gods ($1 toll) to WA 14. Turn left (west) and go 4 miles. Turn left into North Bonneville, then make a quick right onto Cascade Drive. Go 0.4 mile, turn left onto Portage Drive, and look for the trailhead behind the baseball field.

CONTACT: North Bonneville Heritage Trails, (509) 427-8182, northbonneville.net /heritagetrails

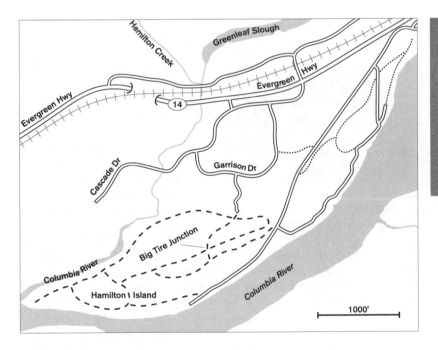

53 FORT CASCADES LOOP

North Bonneville, WA, 46 miles east of downtown Portland

A series of interpretive sites reveals life at a nineteenth-century army outpost in the Columbia River Gorge.

TRAIL	1.5-mile loop
STEEPNESS	Gentle
OTHER USES	Pedestrians only
DOGS	On leash
CONNECTING TRAILS	None
PARK AMENITIES	Restroom, interpretive signs, maps
DISABLED ACCESS	Yes

Long before the completion of the Bonneville Lock and Dam, pioneers who made their way into the Oregon Territory on the Columbia River had to contend with the Cascades of the Columbia, a treacherous 4-mile tumble of rapids in which the river plummeted some 40 feet. To guard the strategic portage road that was cut to bypass this watery hurdle, the military established Fort Cascades in 1855. A self-guided interpretive tour on a near-level trail explores this long-abandoned post, providing a time-traveling stroll in a forest setting along the Columbia River.

Informative maps at the trailhead line out the tour, which features more than a dozen points marking locations of long-gone fish wheels, guardhouses, blacksmith shops, and rail artifacts. The trail starts along the Columbia River with straight-on views of the spillways of the Bonneville Lock and Dam. A series of giant boulders quickly closes in on the path—each of the massive mossy stones was scoured out by a catastrophic flood in 1894 that destroyed the Cascades townsite.

One of the more eye-catching stops is a replica of an Indian petroglyph that was found here (the original now sits at the Skamania Courthouse 6 miles to the east), a reminder that a thriving native village with as many as fourteen houses pre-dated the days of the fort.

In a clearing at the southwest end of the loop, something entirely modern appears: the Bonneville Lock and Dam's Juvenile Fish Monitoring Facility, where hatchery fish are ejected into the river beneath cannon blasts of waters that fend off predatory birds. This system is in stark contrast to the fish wheels that lined the river in the 1890s, scooping out salmon bound for canneries by the thousands.

As you pass back into the forest, you'll see the narrow gauge tracks and sets of wheels from the 1860s Cascade Portage Railroad sitting on the remains of an old roadbed. Near the end of the trail, a lone headstone of a former townsperson seems to speak to the rugged, solitary existence experienced here.

ADDRESS: Dam Access Road, North Bonneville

GETTING THERE: From I-84 E, take exit 44 at Cascade Locks and cross the Bridge of the Gods ($1 toll) to WA 14. Turn left (west), go 3 miles, and turn left onto the Bonneville Dam access road. At the stop sign, turn right onto a fishing access road and continue to the Fort Cascade Historic Site.

CONTACT: US Army Corps of Engineers Portland District, (503) 808-5150, nwp .usace.army.mil

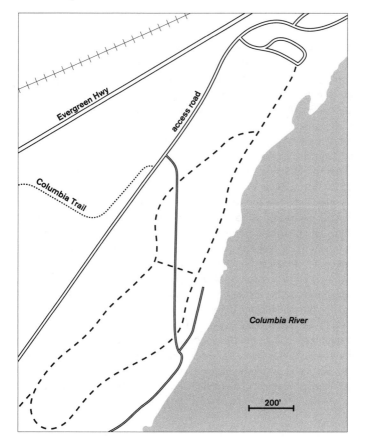

<u>54</u> SAMS WALKER NATURE TRAIL

Stevenson, WA, 40 miles northeast of downtown Portland

Solitude abounds on this quiet loop walk on the site of a former
Columbia River Gorge dairy farm.

TRAIL	1.1-mile loop
STEEPNESS	Gentle
OTHER USES	Pedestrians only
DOGS	On leash
CONNECTING TRAILS	None
PARK AMENITIES	Restrooms, interpretive signs
DISABLED ACCESS	Yes

There may not be a more peaceful hideaway in the Columbia River Gorge. The Sams Walker Nature Trail sits tucked away in Stevenson on 65 acres of oak meadows and forested wetlands that once belonged to a pioneer-era family of German settlers. Threatened with development in the years before the Columbia River Gorge National Scenic Area was established, the site is now under the management of the US Forest Service, which has fashioned a self-guided loop tour blessed with serene views and good opportunities for wildlife sightings.

A post-and-rail fence lines the entrance, evoking the feel of the former farmland. A crushed-gravel trail winds into a sprawling open space known as Grace's Meadow, named for Grace Sams Walker, who bought the land from her father in the 1930s. Nesmith Point and the Rock of Ages peak on the Oregon side of the gorge loom in the distance. Tall non-native grasses planted here to feed dairy cattle are now a hunting ground for red-tailed hawks and great horned owls, which scan the blades for scurrying prey like mice and rabbits. Along the perimeter, scan for black-tailed deer, which gather beneath oak trees to feed on acorns.

Past the meadow's edge, the oak woodland mixes into a line of western red cedars with tangles of branches arching overhead. As the trail winds south toward the river, wetland habitats show signs of restoration work where reed canary grass has been removed to help rehabilitate native sedges.

Blackberry brambles frame a path to a fence-lined overlook with a view of the Columbia River and the 176-foot Horsetail Falls across the river. A pair of benches set beneath cottonwoods and willows makes a lovely spot to take in the scene, and the distant whistle of westbound trains echoing off the gorge walls adds a winsome note as you continue toward a stand of oaks and back to the trailhead.

ADDRESS: Skamina Landing Road, Stevenson, WA

GETTING THERE: From Vancouver, take WA 14 E for 33 miles, turn right onto Skamania Landing Road, and look for the trailhead on the right. A Northwest Forest Pass is required.

CONTACT: US Forest Service, Columbia River Gorge National Scenic Area Headquarters, (541) 308-1700, fs.usda.gov/crgnsa

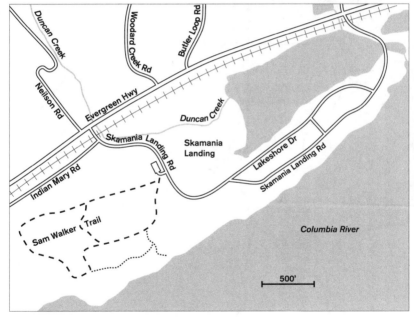

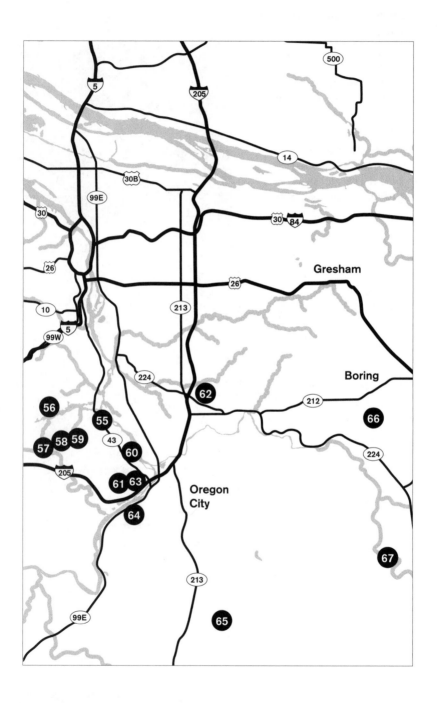

CLACKAMAS COUNTY

<u>55</u> GEORGE ROGERS PARK

Lake Oswego, 8.5 mile south of downtown Portland

A scenic river-hugging stroll awaits on this quiet Willamette River walkway.

TRAIL	2.6 miles round-trip
STEEPNESS	Gentle
OTHER USES	Bicycles
DOGS	On leash
CONNECTING TRAILS	None
PARK AMENITIES	Restrooms, interpretive displays, picnic shelters, kayak and canoe access, sports fields
DISABLED ACCESS	Yes

Now here's a walk that's a real blast. Located along the Willamette River and Oswego Creek, 26-acre George Rogers Park is Lake Oswego's oldest community park and the site of the historic Oswego Iron Furnace, considered the first blast furnace on the Pacific Coast, dating to 1866. Set at the end of a golf green–quality lawn, its imposing stone-and-brick chimney tower looks like a Gothic church. A fantastic series of displays describes the furnace operations, which were prolific: Portland has the second-largest collection of iron-fronted buildings in the country thanks to the ore processed here.

From the lawn, a paved path leads down to an attractive sandy beach where Oswego Creek enters the Willamette River. Ducks bob amid rocks, and even on rainy days you'll likely find beachgoers playing fetch with their dogs.

The main walk starts across Lower Oswego Creek Bridge, where a covered bridge once stood in 1911. The wide blacktop path on the left lines a wooded slope of Oregon ash, maple, and alder and passes a small seasonal waterfall on the right. A pair of wood-railed lookouts provide views down the Willamette and back toward the beach. At 0.3 mile look for a plaque noting the well-preserved Tug Master's House, which was built in 1905 by Crown Willamette Paper Company and sits on the steep slope above.

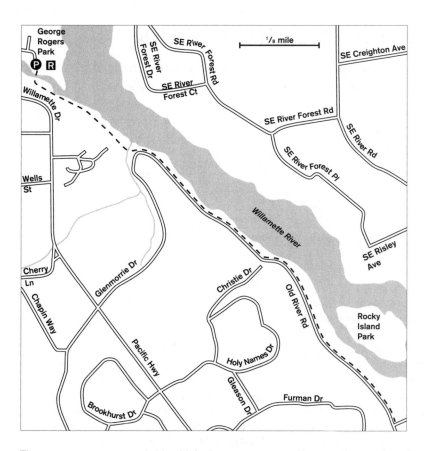

Then cross over a narrow bridge high above a stream and inspect the remains of an old log-hoist building that was used by the paper company.

The car-free path ends here at Old River Road in the upscale Glenmorrie neighborhood, where a series of sculptures denotes the residents' zealous advocacy of trees. (Local homeowners have mapped an official Tree Walk route featuring twenty-four species.) A good walking lane lines Old River Road and traffic is light, so feel free to continue. Ahead the road peeks out at Hagg Island, a river isle full of gnarled trees and bellowing herons. West Linn's Riverwood Place neighborhood, about a mile down the road, marks the turnaround point.

ADDRESS: 611 S State Street, Lake Oswego, OR

GETTING THERE: From OR 43 S (SW Macadam), drive 5.4 miles and look for the park entrance on the left. Continue to the lower lot.

CONTACT: Lake Oswego Parks and Recreation, (503) 675-2549, www.ci.oswego .or.us/parksrec

56 IRON MOUNTAIN PARK

Lake Oswego, 12.5 miles south of downtown Portland

Visit the sight of an old iron mine atop one of the highest points in Lake Oswego.

TRAIL	1.5 miles
STEEPNESS	Moderate
OTHER USES	Horses
DOGS	On leash
CONNECTING TRAILS	None
PARK AMENITIES	Interpretive panels
DISABLED ACCESS	None

Lake Oswego's Iron Mountain takes its name from the historic Prosser iron mine that burrowed into this 450-foot forested mound near SW Lower Boones Ferry Road. Dating to the 1860s, the mine fed Lake Oswego's early dream of becoming the Pittsburgh of the West, producing up to 175 tons of ore a day. Today the trail, which follows an old wagon road (and later a narrow-gauge rail line) used to haul the ore, offers plenty of great views, blazing wildflower displays, and a good workout.

From the trailhead, start out across the base of the slope to the right, slowly rising above Lake Oswego Hunt, a large horse-riding facility. Hoofprints indicate the path is open to equine use. Once upon a time, the trails here even served to train horses for the Clackamas County Sheriff's posse. But you'll need your own internal horsepower to continue the climb.

At 0.5 mile you'll come to a junction. Keep left to rise along steep rocky outcrops and smatterings of oaks, madronas, maples, and in spring, eye-popping blooms of foxgloves and buttercups. Sharp eyes may also spot tiny bits of slag left from the mine twinkling in the sun. By 0.6 mile you'll have come to the high point of the hike, an overlook platform some 400 feet high surveying Cooks Butte Park (Walk #58) and the horse club below. Though the mine shafts located here atop the mountain have long since been closed off, a series of panels details the dangers of daily mine work.

Doubling back is an easy option, but if you'd like to make a loop, keep straight to enter a quiet neighborhood, and head down Glen Eagles Road. At 0.8 mile turn left down a sidewalk onto Wembley Park Road, turn left again onto Twin Fir Road, and make a quick left onto SW Edgemont Road. The trail picks up at the end of this dead-end drive on the right. Follow a zigzag down into the forest, then cross a tiny bridge to go back to the trailhead. In 2016 plans were underway to develop

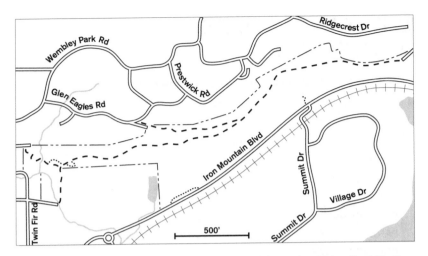

trails to a wetland area in the southeastern edge of the park, which will add to the appeal of this outing.

ADDRESS: Brookside Road, Lake Oswego, OR

GETTING THERE: From I-5 S, take exit 290 onto Lower Boones Ferry Road and go 1.2 miles to Bryant Road. Turn right, then make a quick left onto Upper Drive. Go 0.7 mile, turn left onto Twin Fir Road, go 0.1 mile, and turn right onto Brookside Road. Continue past the "Dead End" sign, where the road turns to dirt. Bear left and look for the trailhead straight ahead, directly behind Lake Oswego Hunt.

CONTACT: Lake Oswego Parks and Recreation, (503) 675-2549, www.ci.oswego .or.us/parksrec

57 BRYANT WOODS NATURE PARK

Lake Oswego, 14 miles south of downtown Portland

A pair of adjoining nature parks provides a green link between Oswego Lake and the Tualatin River.

TRAIL	1.6 miles
STEEPNESS	Gentle
OTHER USES	Pedestrians only
DOGS	On leash
CONNECTING TRAILS	Canal Acres Park
PARK AMENITIES	Small trailhead shelter
DISABLED ACCESS	Yes

Acre for acre, little Bryant Woods Nature Park stacks up against parks even three times its size. At just 17 acres, it safeguards spring-fed wetlands, a meadow ringed by oaks and tall firs, and a historic canal connecting the Tualatin River to Oswego Lake. Adjacent Canal Acres Park adds another 30 acres to the canopy of this neighborhood park

A dirt road beside the Oswego Canal forms the eastern backbone of Bryant Woods. From the trailhead, the wide, level path stretches 0.3 mile beneath shady cottonwoods, maples, and firs. Flanking the road to the left, a meandering network of paths balloons out to the western edge of the park, curving through dense clumps

of forest and passing the park's central meadow before linking to the main canal path at the northern tip of the park.

For a 0.5-mile tour, look for a short boardwalk to the left of the shelter near the trailhead that leads to a rocky single track bowing through ferns, Oregon grapes, and vine maples. A small natural spring provides habitat for northern red-legged frogs and a steady population of ducks. The brush can also hide black-tailed deer.

As the trail loops north, pass through an aisle of firs above the meadow, where camas blooms in the spring. Then curve along bushels of Nootka rose to reach the canal. Cut by Chinese laborers in 1872, the narrow canal was used in 1873 by a sternwheeler steamer, though low river levels soon doomed the channel's usefulness. (Though it still regulates the water level in Oswego Lake.)

To find the river and the canal head gate, cross SW Childs Road into Canal Acres Park. A dirt road lined by maples extends nearly 0.5 mile south to the river. Just a few steps down the road, a new spur turns right on a gravel trail through small firs and connects with the residential West Road. Turn left here to connect to the main dirt road, then walk past a gate to access the head gate on a slow cottonwood-lined bend in the river.

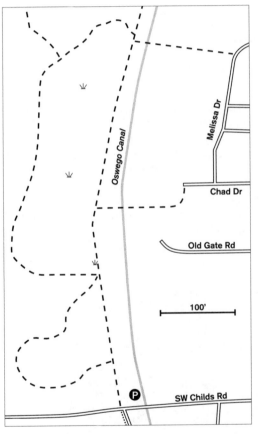

ADDRESS: SW Childs Road and Canal Road, Lake Oswego, OR

GETTING THERE: From I-5 S, take exit 290 onto Lower Boones Ferry Road, and turn left under I-5. Drive 0.7 mile and turn right on Pilkington Road. Go 1 mile and turn left onto SW Childs Road. Go 0.5 mile and look for the park entrance on the left.

CONTACT: Lake Oswego Parks and Recreation, (503) 675-2549, ci.oswego.or.us /parksrec

<u>58</u> COOKS BUTTE PARK

Lake Oswego, 14 miles south of downtown Portland

A rare hilltop forest in Lake Oswego offers a meadow and quiet trails.

TRAIL	Up to 2 miles
STEEPNESS	Moderate
OTHER USES	Mountain bikes
DOGS	On leash; pets not allowed in Stevens Meadows
CONNECTING TRAILS	Stevens Meadows
PARK AMENITIES	Interpretive displays
DISABLED ACCESS	None

Topping out at 718 feet, pine-packed Cooks Butte is one of the highest points in Lake Oswego. Rising just west of the historic Luscher Farm (Walk #59), the 42-acre butte supports a bumper crop of second-growth forest, with big-leaf maples, firs, alders, and a smattering of old fruit trees. Access points dot the lower butte, but the entrance from the Palisades neighborhood, at the end of Palisades Crest Drive, provides direct access to the summit and an easy mile-long loop.

From the trailhead, you can walk straight up a wide gravel road, passing a water-storage unit hidden in the trees, to a summit-top meadow with a thick ring of firs. Soak up the tranquil setting on a boulder-lined bench, then follow the sign for the Cooks Butte Trail to zigzag down a tunnel of alders. At the marked junction, with a posted trail map, you can continue downhill and exit to neighborhood

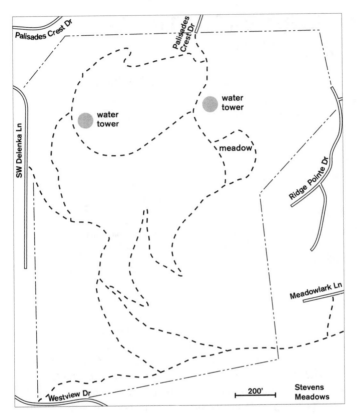

streets that connect to Stevens Meadows, where a 0.5-mile loop circles the open pasture near a large historic barn and Pecan Creek.

Heading uphill from the marked junction keeps you in the forest. Rising along a section lined with nurse logs, the path meets a wide gravel lane set below a second water-storage tank. Up to the right, a line of mossy boulders marks a side trail to the top of the tank, which doubles as a forest overlook. Atop the rail-lined reservoir, views are limited, but it's an excellent treetop-level location to listen for resident songbirds. Continue uphill on the gravel lane to reach the trailhead starting point.

ADDRESS: Palisades Crest Drive, Lake Oswego, OR

GETTING THERE: From I-205, take the exit for Stafford Road. Drive 1.7 miles to Overlook Drive and turn left. Go 0.9 mile and turn left onto Westview Drive. Go 0.3 mile, turn left onto Palisades Crest, and drive uphill for 0.5 mile to reach the trailhead.

CONTACT: Lake Oswego Parks and Recreation, (503) 675-2549, ci.oswego.or.us /parksrec

<u>59</u> STAFFORD BASIN TRAIL– LUSCHER FARM

Lake Oswego, 10 miles south of downtown Portland

Take a pastoral walk through the historic Luscher Farm and orchards, and see a monument of one of the state's beloved poets.

TRAIL	2.4 miles
STEEPNESS	Gentle
OTHER USES	Bicycles
DOGS	On leash; dog park at Hazelia Field
CONNECTING TRAILS	None
PARK AMENITIES	Restrooms at Hazelia Field, portable restroom at Luscher Farm, interpretive signs, artwork
DISABLED ACCESS	Yes

Some walks produce blisters—this one may result in a green thumb.

Following an easy paved course through a pastoral setting, walkers visit the historic Luscher Farm and pass into the rural boundaries of Lake Oswego. Once a dairy farm with prized Holstein cows, the farm is now maintained by the City of Lake Oswego as part of a unique 47-acre site offering a slate of educational and public garden plots, including a nationally renowned collection of clematis flowers. The property also features nearly 4 acres of wetland habitat.

Depart from an interpretive display just beyond the Hazelia Field dog park, following a curving path 0.2 mile to the Luscher Farm entrance, near the property's Queen Anne–style farmhouse. Here you'll also find the Rogerson Clematis Garden. The 1,700 individual plants representing 735 species make this one of the top collections in the nation. Just ahead a series of 180 community garden plots are one of the hottest tickets in town, with lottos held to snag empty lots.

The path continues past the farm, buffered from Rosemont Road by a line of mammoth trees, including a sequoia noted as a Lake Oswego Heritage Tree. At approximately 0.5 mile, walkers come to a stone obelisk monument to William Stafford, Oregon's famed poet laureate and a former Lake Oswego resident. Take a moment to read the inscribed poem, "The Well Rising." Down from the monument, a small loop section encircles a sprawling lawn. Continue around and make a right at a junction that leads past a small pear and apple orchard.

Ahead the terrain becomes hilly. Continue down a sunny slope set beneath a fence line, momentarily skirting Rosemont Road. Past a creek, follow the S curve

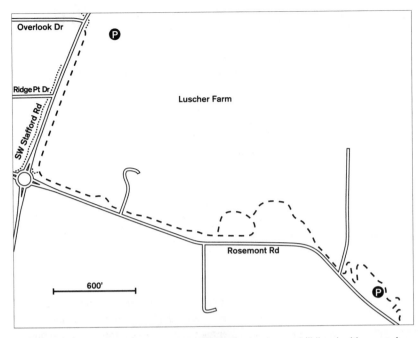

back up a hill lined with a patch of alder trees before ending at an alternate trailhead off Rosemont Road, where a circular path overlooks Oswego Hills Vineyard and Winery.

ADDRESS: 17800 Stafford Road, Lake Oswego, OR

GETTING THERE: On OR 43 S, go 6 miles and turn right on McVey Avenue. Go 0.8 mile, continue on Stafford Road, and turn left on Overlook Drive. Hazelia Field at Luscher Farm will be on the left.

CONTACT: Lake Oswego Parks and Recreation, (503) 534-5284, ci.oswego.or.us /parksrec

<u>60</u> MARY S. YOUNG STATE PARK

West Linn, 13 miles south of downtown Portland

Stroll down a paved path to the Willamette River in this small state park in West Linn.

TRAIL	1 mile
STEEPNESS	Gentle to moderate
OTHER USES	Pedestrians only
DOGS	On leash; two off-leash areas
CONNECTING TRAILS	None
PARK AMENITIES	Restrooms, group picnic shelter, off-leash dog areas, soccer fields, interpretive signs
DISABLED ACCESS	Yes

Mary S. Young moved to Lake Oswego in 1922 and devoted the next 50 years of her life to her community. Her advocacy ranged from beautifying local parks to scanning the night sky for enemy planes with the civil defense during World War II. Apparently, she could also hold a grudge. Local lore maintains that after receiving a speeding ticket in Lake Oswego in her red Ford Thunderbird, she chose to bequeath 130 acres of forestland she owned along the Willamette River to the State of Oregon instead of her adopted city. *Ouch.* Her generous gift has been open to everyone (including Lake Oswegoans) in the form of her namesake state park since 1973.

Of the 8 miles' worth of trails, the 1.5-mile wood-chip Heron Creek Loop Trail is the longest, forming the park's boxy perimeter. The northern portion feels wilder, with large maples and alders and rushing Heron Creek, while the southern section passes soccer fields and a popular off-leash pet area. To get straight to the main attraction—the river—follow the 0.8-mile Riverside Loop (0.6 mile of which are paved) down to the Willamette.

After dropping through an abundance of maples and firs, the path meets a turnoff for Cedar Island Trail, which provides seasonal access (spring through fall) to Cedar Island across a floating metal bridge. Officially its

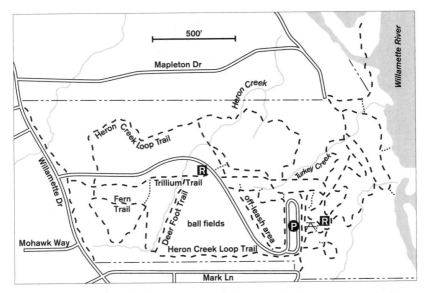

own park, this 14-acre islet has stone-lined beaches, fishing platforms, and a huge pond frequented by bass anglers.

The Riverside Loop continues on an unpaved course to the right, through a low-lying clearing that skirts the river. Here you can scramble over, under, or around fallen trunks and claim your own rocky finger jutting into the river. Across a footbridge, a sandy beach doubles as another sanctioned off-leash dog area.

At 0.6 mile, the trail heads up, passing a stream to loop back to the main paved path. The fairly steep climb out can be mitigated by turning off on a side trail to pause at a mossy stone plaza overlooking the river before proceeding up to the trailhead.

ADDRESS: 19900 Willamette Drive, West Linn, OR

GETTING THERE: From OR 43 S, drive 11 miles and look for the park entrance on the left. Pass the first parking area on the left, and continue 0.2 mile past soccer fields on your right to reach the main parking lot.

CONTACT: West Linn Parks and Recreation, (503) 557-4700, westlinnoregon.gov /parksrec

61 WILDERNESS PARK

West Linn, 16 miles south of downtown Portland

Walk in the shadows of giant Douglas firs in this peaceful West Linn preserve.

TRAIL	Up to 1.5 miles
STEEPNESS	Moderate
OTHER USES	Pedestrians only
DOGS	On leash
CONNECTING TRAILS	None
PARK AMENITIES	None
DISABLED ACCESS	None

While it's not full of true wilderness, 51-acre Wilderness Park does pack in very large Douglas firs—lots of them. They appear spread out across an imposing 600-foot mound rising above West Linn High School and provide a wonderful sense of a deep-woods escape. Interspersed with the giants are spindly vine maple, salal, holly, pacific elderberry, and bright blooms of wood violets.

You can just about wander at will here, but keep in mind that trails aren't marked and there are several informal user paths. Rising up to the right side of the ridge to the east will let you funnel down toward a main path that borders Clark Street.

From the parking lot, rise up a wide dirt path, and turn right at the first junction, continuing on a slope with an avalanche of ferns spilling down to the parking lot, visible to the right. Keep right, continuing on the ridge sprinkled with starlike little flowers, then turn left, heading uphill, by a set of wooden steps (which tread steeply downhill, returning to the parking lot). As the trail winds left, pass a double-trunked Douglas fir, and keep straight along the high point of the ridge, around 575 feet tall. At 0.5 mile hang a left and connect with a wider path, which drops across the slope toward Clark Street to a closed-off parking area that's piled with thinned timber. Pick up the trail again to the left of the lot. This wide trail then drops down to the main lot.

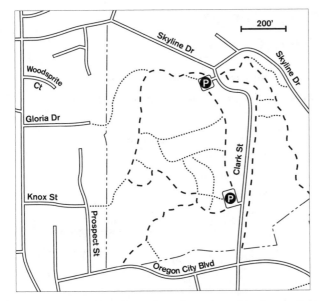

Just across Clark Street from the main parking lot, another short network of trails treads a lower ravine offering a few tree-obscured views of forested buttes rising to the northeast of Portland. You'll also find another fun, steep log staircase that zips back to the road. At the eastern corner of this lower slope, you can also follow a track out of the park, behind the high school, for 0.5 mile to connect with Camassia Natural Area (Walk #63).

ADDRESS: 22101 Clark Street, West Linn, OR

GETTING THERE: From OR 43 S, drive 8 miles to West Linn, and turn right on West A Street. Go 0.5 mile and turn right onto Skyline Drive. Go 0.5 mile, turn left onto Clark Street, and look for the park entrance on the left.

CONTACT: West Linn Parks and Recreation, (503) 557-4700, westlinnoregon.gov /parksrec

<u>62</u> MOUNT TALBERT NATURE PARK

Clackamas, 13 miles southeast of downtown Portland

An inviting woodland refuge wraps around the flanks of Portland's tallest volcanic butte.

TRAIL	4 miles total; 2.7 miles as described here
STEEPNESS	Moderate to steep
OTHER USES	Pedestrians only
DOGS	Not allowed
CONNECTING TRAILS	None
PARK AMENITIES	Restrooms, group picnic shelters, interpretive displays
DISABLED ACCESS	Mather Road Trailhead

The largest of the east side's string of undeveloped volcanic buttes, Mount Talbert rises 750 feet above a heavily urbanized corner of Clackamas County. Run by Metro, the 216-acre park serves as a kind of "break glass in case of emergency" woodland escape for anyone in the I-205 vicinity.

The slopes are encircled by a 4-mile trail system that tours a range of habitats, including oak woodland and prairie under active restoration. (Douglas firs are thinned in these areas to let slower-growing oaks flourish.) On the northern flanks, Mount Scott Creek trickles beneath salal and red huckleberry blooms and supports a salmon population. Tall firs, maples, and sword ferns line the butte's lush western reaches. Black-tailed deer thrive along with foxes, coyotes, and other rarer

critters like rubber boa snakes. In spring, the butte is a virtual atoll for migratory songbirds like warblers and vireos. Douglas firs have also been vigorously scored by hairy woodpeckers.

A thick tree canopy extends uniformly around the peak, which limits views (even from the lofty summit) and can make orienting yourself a challenge. But signposts with maps at trail junctions aid in navigating your route.

The easygoing nearly 2-mile Park Loop Trail provides the most level

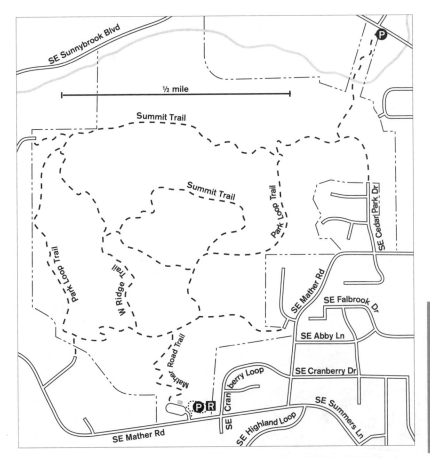

walking, encircling the butte. From this you can connect to the Summit Trail, along with spurs to four separate trailheads. Hard-packed trails all around make for sturdy walking even in the rainy season. At the Mather Road Trailhead, circle the short ADA-compliant loop for a chance to see brilliant blooms of camas, Oregon iris, and checkermallow.

ADDRESS: 10945 SE Mather Road, Clackamas, OR

GETTING THERE: From I-205 S, take exit 14 onto Sunnyside Road, toward SE Sunnybrook Boulevard. Turn left onto SE Sunnybrook Boulevard, and make a quick right onto SE 97th Avenue. Continue 1.2 miles and turn left on SE Mather Road. Look for the trailhead on the left.

CONTACT: Metro, (503) 665-4995, oregonmetro.gov

<u>63</u> CAMASSIA NATURAL AREA

West Linn, 13.5 miles south of downtown Portland

Ancient rocks, wildflowers, and sweeping views sprout from this Nature Conservancy site rising above the Willamette River.

TRAIL	1 mile
STEEPNESS	Gentle
OTHER USES	Pedestrians only
DOGS	Not allowed
CONNECTING TRAILS	None
PARK AMENITIES	None
DISABLED ACCESS	None

Fifteen thousand years ago, walkers would have been well-advised to steer clear of this small West Linn natural area. Repeated deluges of debris-laden water, unleashed during the prehistoric Missoula Floods, scoured through the Willamette Valley, jettisoning giant rocks and leaving them marooned here. Known in geologic parlance as glacial erratics, these black-and-white speckled rocks now form the literal cornerstones of a 27-acre Nature Conservancy preserve.

Self-guided tour maps are available at the trailhead and lead visitors on a gentle 1-mile loop among these interloping rocks and to the edges of the basalt cliffs rising over the Willamette River. Surrounding the characteristic rocks are open meadows sprinkled with scrubby Oregon white oaks and Pacific madronas, representing a habitat that has all but vanished from the Willamette Valley. (Yet another reason this area became the Nature Conservancy's first Oregon preserve in 1962.)

Camassia also has a more delicate side: the area cradles more than three hundred species of plants, including robust showings of the namesake camas flowers each April and May. Exceedingly rare varieties also bloom, like the white rock larkspur, which occurs in only a handful places worldwide. Boardwalks lead through the most ecologically sensitive areas, including forested wetlands.

The mix of meadows, ponds, and trees, including stands of quaking aspen, attract a mix of birdlife, from wood ducks to golden-crowned kinglets to screech owls. (In the past, ospreys have also nested on a cell tower visible to the north of the reserve grounds.) Along the eastern edges of the perimeter, the exposed bedrock scraped off by the cataclysmic floods provides a dramatic stage to take in views of Mount Hood.

ADDRESS: 5000 Walnut Street, West Linn, OR

GETTING THERE: From I-205 S, take exit 8 for West Linn, and turn left to cross under the highway. Turn uphill onto Willamette Falls Drive, continue to the left, and turn right (uphill) onto Sunset Avenue. Take the first right onto Walnut Street, and look for the entrance at the end of the street.

CONTACT: The Nature Conservancy, (503) 802-8100, nature.org

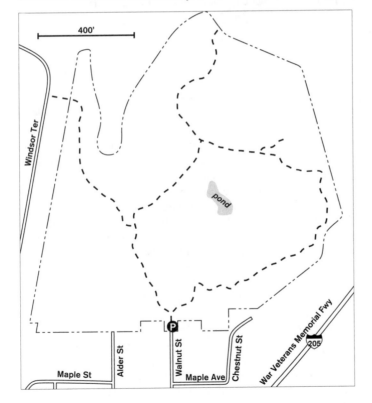

<u>64</u> CANEMAH BLUFF NATURE PARK

Oregon City, 14 miles southeast of downtown Portland

Rich wildflower blooms, deep cultural history, and astounding Willamette River views await on an easy loop around this blufftop natural area.

TRAIL	Approximately 1.2 miles
STEEPNESS	Gentle to moderate
OTHER USES	Pedestrians only
DOGS	Not allowed
CONNECTING TRAILS	None
PARK AMENITIES	Restrooms, interpretive signs, playground, basketball court
DISABLED ACCESS	Yes

Occupying a rocky bench birthed from prehistoric landslides and lava flows, Canemah Bluff sits 0.5 mile upriver from Willamette Falls. Native tribes who gathered to fish at the falls used the oak- and fir-capped bluff as an encampment area. ("Canemah" or "kanim" translates to "canoe place.") Later, roads were cut here by settlers portaging around the falls. These old lanes also access the pioneer-era Canemah Cemetery, which still lines the edge of the park.

Yet in 2017, it's Canemah's newer features that get your attention. From the trailhead in Canemah Children's Park, the new Camas Spring Trail, an ADA-compliant crushed-gravel path leads 0.1 mile through a restored prairie meadow filled with camas, buttercups, and lupines to a new lookout over the Willamette River, and freshly signed trails throughout the natural area help orient walkers. From the overlook, the trail enters a shady mix of firs and alders, leading to the Canemah Historic Pioneer Cemetery Road. Follow the road to the right toward jumbles of boulders tossed here during the catastrophic Missoula Floods. Within 0.5 mile you'll reach the cemetery.

To the left of the graveyard, follow the Spur Trail curving among the sword ferns to the left, and leading to a connection with the Licorice Fern Trail. Here, you can turn left to loop back to the main cemetery road and the trailhead. The second option: turn right, and in a few paces keep left on the Licorice Fern Trail, which wends beneath a forested ridge line for 0.4-miles. This path exits into the Canemah neighborhood at a new trailhead near the intersection of 5th Avenue and 5th Place. To reenter the natural area, turn left onto 5th Avenue, following a

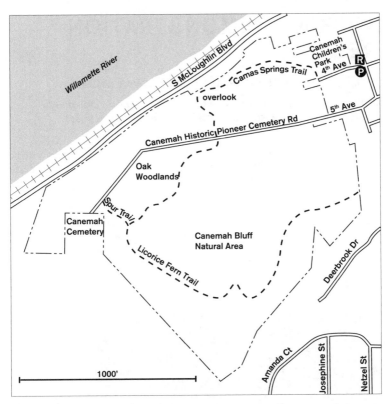

sign for the historic cemetery, and proceed down the cemetery road to an inter-section with the Frog Pond Trail, which drops down back to the main trailhead.

ADDRESS: 815 4th Avenue, Oregon City, OR

GETTING THERE: From I-205, take exit 9. Head south on Highway 99 (McLoughlin Boulevard) for 0.9 mile, passing through a tunnel, and turn left onto S 2nd Street. In one block turn right onto High Street and then bear right on 5th Avenue (which turns into Miller Street) into the Canemah Historic District. At the stop sign, turn left onto 4th Avenue. Park at Canemah Children's Park.

CONTACT: Metro, (503) 797-1545, oregonmetro.gov

<u>65</u> HOPKINS DEMONSTRATION FOREST

Oregon City, 29 miles southeast of downtown Portland

A stroll-through is unique in this 140-acre habitat that provides plenty of solitude along with lessons in sustainable forestry practices.

TRAIL	Up to 5 miles
STEEPNESS	Moderate to steep
OTHER USES	Pedestrians only
DOGS	On leash
CONNECTING TRAILS	None
PARK AMENITIES	Restrooms, interpretive kiosk, trail maps
DISABLED ACCESS	None

Meant to exemplify sustainable forestry practices, the 140 acres of timberland at Hopkins Demonstration Forest are a woodsy workshop for school-age kids, Oregon State University extension programs, forestry officials, and private land owners. Managed by the nonprofit Forests Forever Inc., the property is divided into twenty management units that are actively harvested and replanted. There are stands designated for utility poles (an especially valuable timber crop) and plots thinned for Christmas trees and decorative boughs. There's an orchard of red alders. Other areas are more experimental, with a variety of species and ages.

The diverse portfolio of trees, along with a meandering creek and a pair of ponds set in a deep gulch, add up to an exceptionally pretty place to spend a few hours exploring. The demonstration forest is open to the public 7 days a week, and you can stroll 5 miles of trails that wander freely through the forest.

The trailhead offers an interpretive kiosk with trail maps and loads of information on the forest. The central Grouse Hollow Road stretches through the forest east to west, and most trails loop off this main path.

For a look at the forest's educational side, follow the Hopkins Trail down to an outdoor classroom area and shelter beneath shady western red cedars. From here Low Gear Road leads up to a clearing, where you veer down the Shortcut Trail (crossing over Grouse Hollow Road) to reach the West Loop Watershed Trail at 0.7 mile. Ahead a fence-lined boardwalk offers wonderful views of Little Buckner Creek flowing amid a mossy ravine. Continue to trace the creek along the Middle Loop Watershed Trail beside more western red cedars and alders, and find a return route by turning left on Up Creek Road. Then follow Grouse Hollow Road approximately 0.5 mile back to the trailhead.

ADDRESS: 16750 S Brockway Road, Oregon City, OR

GETTING THERE: From I-205 S, take exit 10 to Highway 213 S. Go 7.5 miles to Spangler Road and turn left. Go 2 miles to S Brockway Road and turn right. Follow the signs to the parking lot.

CONTACT: Hopkins Demonstration Forest, (503) 632-2150, demonstrationforest.org

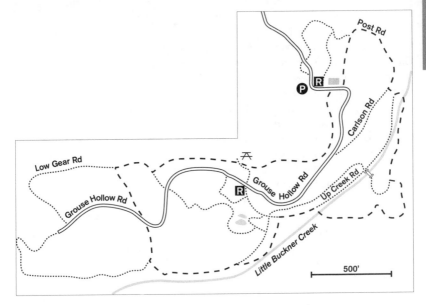

<u>66</u> CAZADERO TRAIL

Boring, 24 miles southeast of downtown Portland

Peacefulness abounds on this little-known rail-to-trail path tracing Deep Creek.

TRAIL	3 miles one way
STEEPNESS	Gentle
OTHER USES	Bicycles
DOGS	On leash
CONNECTING TRAILS	None
PARK AMENITIES	None
DISABLED ACCESS	Yes

The little-known Cazadero Trail awaits just across Highway 212 from the Boring Station Trailhead of the Springwater Corridor, which now provides a completed 21-mile link between Portland and Boring. And where the Springwater's pavement ends, the Cazadero's wildness begins. Tracking the former course of the Oregon Water Power and Railway Company rail line (abandoned in 1943), the gravel roadbed borders Deep Creek and descends slowly into a forest canyon lined with western red cedars, Douglas firs, ash, and cottonwoods.

Well removed from urban bustle, the wide swath cut by the canyon here is noted as a prime wildlife corridor between the forested buttes of Gresham and the Clackamas River, harboring black-tailed deer, foxes, coyotes, and other restless mammals. The streamside forest is also an outstanding habitat for larger birds such as northern flickers, red-tailed hawks, and turkey vultures. Peregrine falcons have also been seen nesting along bluff tops.

Civilization isn't totally lost though. Within the first mile you'll catch glimpses of Mountain View Golf Course across Deep Creek to the south. A power line also trails overhead, and you'll wander past a hillside horse pasture. The cacophonous Deep Creek is a near-constant companion. Just short of a mile, a large streamside area set beneath a grove of western red cedars provides an inviting spot to

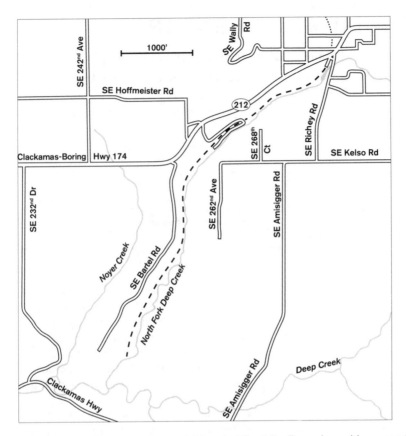

inspect the boulder-strewn current. A bend at the 1.5-mile mark provides a good overlook of the creek's meandering path.

As of 2016 the trail ends 3 miles in, at a bench-lined wooden fence near the North Fork of Deep Creek. Plans are imminent to provide a connection to Boring's Barton Park, which is just 0.5 mile ahead, across Highway 224. From there, the path will connect to Timber Park along the Clackamas River. One day it may also reach the Pacific Crest Trail near Mount Hood, providing the ultimate nature escape route.

ADDRESS: Highway 212 and SE Richey Road, Boring, OR

GETTING THERE: From I-205 S, take exit 14 for Sunnyside Road and turn left. Go 5.7 miles and turn left onto Highway 212. Continue 4 miles to SE Richey Road and turn right into a gravel parking lot (behind the Shell gas station). Additional parking is available across Highway 212 at the Boring Station Trailhead.

CONTACT: Clackamas County Parks, (503) 742-4414, clackamas.us/parks

<u>67</u> MILO MCIVER BAT TRAIL

Estacada, 26 miles southeast of downtown Portland

Learn about one the state's rarest colonies of bats, and take in gorgeous Mount Hood views.

TRAIL	1-mile loop
STEEPNESS	Gentle
OTHER USES	Horses
DOGS	On leash
CONNECTING TRAILS	None
PARK AMENITIES	Restrooms, campground, disc-golf course, boat launch, interpretive displays
DISABLED ACCESS	None

In the summer of 1970, one of the strangest scenes in Oregon history played out at Milo McIver State Park. With a massive antiwar protest brewing in Portland, then-governor Tom McCall did the unthinkable. He threw a party. Dubbed Vortex I: A Biodegradable Festival of Life, it was meant to divert youngsters to the park for three days of sex, drugs, and rock 'n' roll, while the state picked up the tab for music, food, and even transportation. Stranger still, the whole thing went off without a hitch.

With some historical perspective, the idea of a Milo McIver State Park trail devoted to bats seems rather tame. The 950-acre park, which sits nuzzled up to the Clackamas River (and is best known for its scenic disc-golf course), is home to at least six species of bats, including little brown bats, big brown bats, and silver-haired bats. But one group stands out—a colony of Townsend's big-eared

bats was discovered in a former horse barn set at the edge of a large meadow in the park. This summer roost is now considered one of the few nursery colonies in Oregon used by bats listed as a species of special concern.

A 1-mile loop trail circles the prairie meadow, leading to the edge of the large weathered bat barn. Self-guided tour maps are

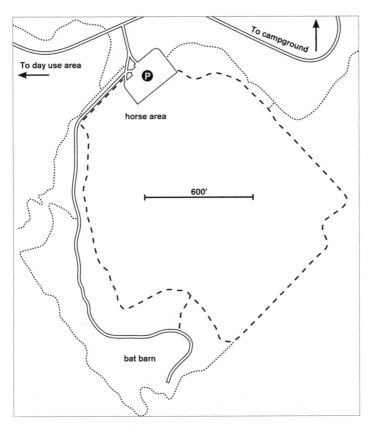

To campground

To day use area

P

horse area

600'

bat barn

available at the trailhead and detail fascinating bat factoids ("Bats eat 500 mosquitoes every hour!").

Along with the barn, several bat houses made by Boy Scouts line the trail, providing roosts for up to fifty bats. And early morning strolls reveal the park's other residents, like solitary coyotes scouting the field, along with bat-eating owls and red-tailed hawks. Ringed with Douglas firs, the meadow also boasts outstanding Mount Hood views. The loop doubles as a unique equestrian training course that includes miniature suspension bridges and seesaws.

ADDRESS: 24101 S Entrance Road, Estacada, OR

GETTING THERE: From I-205 S, take exit 12A to merge onto OR 224 E. Go 3.5 miles and turn right to stay on OR 224 E. Go 1.1 miles and bear right on Market Road 39. This road becomes S Springwater Road. Continue 9.2 miles and look for the park entrance on the left. To reach the bat trail, continue to the Riverside day-use area, following signs for the equestrian trailhead.

CONTACT: Oregon State Parks, (503) 630-7150, oregonstateparks.org

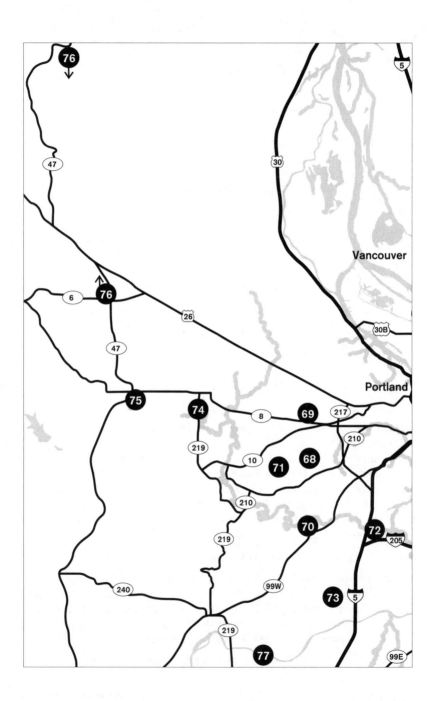

WASHINGTON
COUNTY

WASHINGTON COUNTY

68 FANNO CREEK GREENWAY TRAIL

Beaverton, 12 miles southwest of downtown Portland

Head into the suburban wilds on this popular greenway trail that visits a flourishing wetland habitat.

TRAIL	1.8 miles one way
STEEPNESS	Gentle
OTHER USES	Bicycles
DOGS	On leash
CONNECTING TRAILS	None
PARK AMENITIES	Playgrounds, interpretive displays, disc-golf course
DISABLED ACCESS	Yes

The willow- and oak-lined lawns of Beaverton's 87-acre Greenway Park provide a diverse showcase for one of the region's hallmark multiuse paths, the Fanno Creek Greenway Trail. Linking Southwest Portland and Tigard, the trail follows its namesake stream nearly 12 miles in partially connected segments. Along this 1.8-mile stretch, walkers discover the historical roots of the creek's development at the nineteenth-century farmhouse of Augustus Fanno, who settled here in the 1840s, and inspect the handiwork of some of the trail's more recent pioneers—urban beavers.

From the SW Denney Road Trailhead, dip south along a slender seasonal marsh, which fills with wintering Canada geese and a variety of ducks. Fanno Creek trickles to the right beneath rows of Oregon ash. At 0.7 mile cross SW Hall Boulevard to Greenway Park, where Fanno Creek's robust wetland habitat blends with a popular disc-golf course and a series of play structures.

Just inside the park, the Fanno Farmhouse, a distinguished cream-colored New England–style cottage built in 1859, now looks quite out of place tucked amid its modern office-park surroundings, but it's a rare visceral link to the area's agricultural heritage. (A successful farmer, Fanno was known as the Onion King.)

A resident family of beavers has done its best to revert the developed landscape to a more rustic setting. Their handiwork, visible 0.3 mile past SW Hall Boulevard, has flooded an interior loop path and marooned portions of the disc-golf course.

You're not likely to see these nocturnal engineers, but you will need to navigate around marked detours, including a submerged portion near the walk's end at SW Scholls Ferry Road that swarms with candy-red dragonflies and squiggly tadpoles.

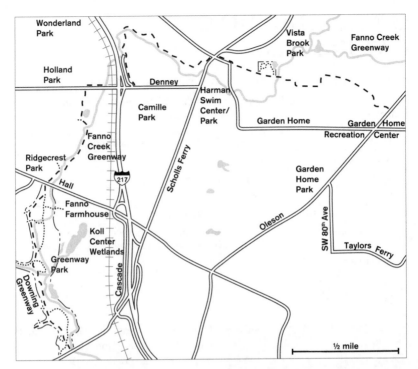

Plan extra time to bird-watch around Creekside Marsh, which borders the disc-golf area 0.4 mile past SW Hall Boulevard. The sedges and cattails here are ideal for Virginia rails, spotted towhees, song sparrows, and belted kingfishers.

ADDRESS: SW Denney Road, just west of Highway 217, Beaverton, OR

GETTING THERE: From US 26 W, take exit 69A for OR 217 S. Drive 2.7 miles and take exit 3 for SW Denney Road. Look for the trailhead on the left.

CONTACT: Tualatin Hills Parks and Recreation, (503) 645-6433, thprd.org

69 TUALATIN HILLS NATURE PARK

Beaverton, 8 miles southwest of downtown Portland

A diverse array of habitats converge in this 222-acre Beaverton preserve, which is accessible via MAX Light Rail.

TRAIL	Up to 5 miles; 2 miles as described here
STEEPNESS	Gentle
OTHER USES	Bicycles on paved trails only
DOGS	Not allowed
CONNECTING TRAILS	Westside Regional Trail
PARK AMENITIES	Visitor center, restrooms, guided nature walks, interpretive displays, direct access to MAX Blue Line
DISABLED ACCESS	Yes

Often referred to as a mosaic of habitats, this 222-acre Beaverton park entwines oak woodlands, ponderosa pine forests, wetlands, streams, meadows, and ponds. The unique convergence wasn't lost on city officials, who had originally envisioned a state park designation (St. Mary's Forest State Park) in 1978. Limited state funds, however, meant the idea was scrapped. Luckily, within a few years, the City of Beaverton pursued scaled-back plans for the current nature park.

Stretches of paved paths, like the 1.5-mile Vine Maple Trail, which travels from east to west through the center of the park, make it an ideal accessible, all-weather destination. Connecting loops of natural surface trails deliver more solitude, with tall stands of timber and carpets of springtime blooms.

The staffed nature center at the west side of the Vine Maple Trail serves as the main jumping-off point. Maps are readily available, and the park staff will get you up to speed on which trails might be mud logged.

To visit the extensive marsh habitat, follow the Oak Trail, which borders mossy trees. Ahead several boardwalks act like front-row seats for a concerto of Pacific tree frogs. To loop back to the center of the park, follow the gravel-surfaced

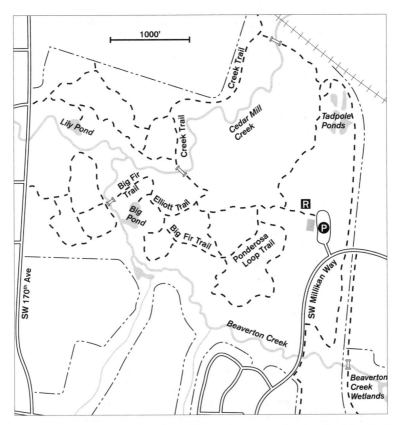

Creek Trail, passing by tall reeds and into a dramatic collection of tall firs that feel beamed in from the wilds of the Mount Hood National Forest.

Back on the Vine Maple Trail, make a quick loop on the unpaved Elliot and Big Fir Trails, which feature the largest trees in the park and brilliant wildflowers, starting with trilliums in the early spring, followed by other showy specimens like starflowers and Indian pipe. Near the visitor center, the Ponderosa Loop Trail offers a look at the rare combination of massive oak trees and soggy wetlands.

If you've been touring on a chilly day, stop back into the nature center, where a fireside library makes an inviting spot to reference local wildlife guides.

ADDRESS: 15655 SW Millikan Way, Beaverton, OR

GETTING THERE: From US 26 W, take exit 67 for SW Murray Boulevard, and turn left onto Murray. Turn right onto Millikan Way, continue through SW 154th Avenue, and look for the park entrance on the right. Light rail access is also available via the Merlo Road / SW 158th Avenue MAX Station.

CONTACT: Tualatin Hills Parks and Recreation, (503) 629-6350, thprd.org

70 TUALATIN RIVER NATIONAL WILDLIFE REFUGE

Sherwood, 15 miles southwest of downtown Portland

Celebrate the twenty-fifth anniversary of one of the country's few federal urban wildlife refuges, with sightings of geese, eagles, otters, and other wild residents.

TRAIL	1 mile one way, open year-round; 3 additional miles open from May to September
STEEPNESS	Gentle
OTHER USES	Pedestrians only
DOGS	Not allowed
CONNECTING TRAILS	None
PARK AMENITIES	Visitor center, gift shop, interpretive museum, rest rooms, spotting scopes, group shelter, bird blind (by reservation)
DISABLED ACCESS	Yes

In 2017 the Tualatin River National Wildlife Refuge celebrates 25 years since being founded as one of the few federal urban wildlife refuges in the country. (Ridgefield National Wildlife Refuge is also among them—see Walks #38 and #39.) By any measure, the refuge is a winner. Since this swath of former Tualatin Valley dairy and onion farms was converted into the sprawling 1,800-acre complex, some two hundred species of birds, fifty kinds of mammals, and twenty-five reptiles and amphibians have been recorded here. In winter up to fifty thousand geese have been seen on site.

The refuge is split into five separate units that spread across 1,800 acres, but only the 450-acre Atfálat'i Unit is accessible to the public. A large state-of-the-art visitor center opened in 2008 and features exhibits, a nature store, and a full slate of educational activities like guided walks. They'll even loan you binoculars. A 1-mile trail is open year-round and is gentle enough for even the

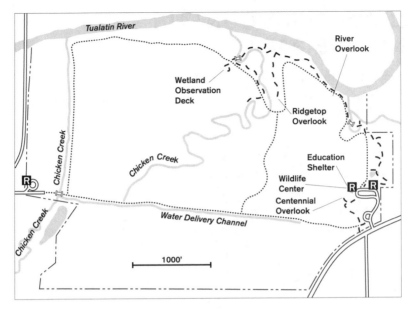

littlest walkers. Along the path, you'll visit oak savanna, riparian forest, creeks, and ponds. From May to September, 3 more miles of gravel access roads are open to the public, allowing further walks around the wetland's western perimeter, where Chicken Creek cuts across the refuge.

Along the year-round path, you might encounter a biologist examining tiny refuge inhabitants like caddisflies and fairy shrimp at a pond study site, or see a hawk gravitating to a large oak tree. At a river-platform overlook, you might spot otters poking their whiskers out of the water. After entering a forest, the path ends at a large curving metal platform set at the edge of a wetland. If you've ever thought about purchasing binoculars, this could be the breaking point. Geese and ducks come in waves, and in the distance eagles skulk on large snags in the lake. On the trip out, look for a short but steep side trail up to a narrow ridgetop that is enclosed by a metal railing and points out toward the water, giving the sense of being on the prow of a ship.

ADDRESS: 19255 SW Pacific Highway, Sherwood, OR

GETTING THERE: From I-5 S, take exit 294 for OR 99 W (toward Tigard/Newberg). Drive 6.5 miles and look for the entrance on the right.

CONTACT: US Fish and Wildlife Service, Tualatin River National Wildlife Refuge, (503) 625-5944, fws.gov/tualatinriver

71 COOPER MOUNTAIN NATURE PARK

Beaverton, 16 miles southwest of Portland

On a high slope above the Tualatin Valley, you'll find oak prairies, wildflowers, and mountain views.

TRAIL	Up to 3 miles
STEEPNESS	Moderate to steep
OTHER USES	Pedestrians only
DOGS	Not allowed
CONNECTING TRAILS	None
PARK AMENITIES	Restrooms, interpretive displays, art installations, play structure, demonstration garden, nature center, nature walks, classes
DISABLED ACCESS	0.75-mile loop trail

Formed of old basalt flows that folded on top of each other, Cooper Mountain rises some 800 feet above the Tualatin Valley in southwest Beaverton. From the trailhead you can stare out at a vast panorama of the Chehalem Mountains across the valley.

Officially opened for use in 2009 by Metro, the 3-mile system of trails forms a series of well-signed loops that dip below the trailhead and into a mix of slope-side habitats, including oak woodlands, prairies, and cool conifer-dominated forests. The slope's sunny southern exposure means wildflowers start popping by late February and early March, making this a great place to shake off the winter blues. Oregon iris and endangered species like golden paintbrush and white rock lark-spur are just a few of the seasonal favorites. Open vistas and well-spaced trees make for easy bird-watching. Art installations, called listening trumpets, that swivel to help you home in on bird chatter add a touch of whimsy.

Considering that all the trails head downhill, you'll need to remember a twist on an old adage: what goes *down*, must come *up*. It's about a 1-mile walk to the base of the hill, which you can reach by taking the Cooper Mountain Loop in either direction. Along the lower reaches of this trail, a small man-made pond has become a boon to local wildlife; most notably, rare northern red-legged frogs now breed here.

The climb out is taxing but not punishing. On hot days, plan a route back up the Blacktail Way (which connects with the Cooper Mountain Loop). This trail rises between a draw covered with large oaks, madronas, and evergreens, and

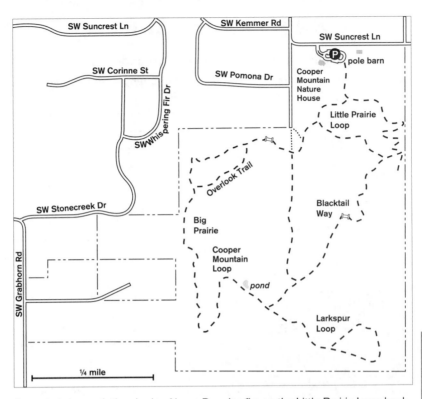

then winds beneath the shade of large Douglas firs on the Little Prairie Loop back to the trailhead.

ADDRESS: 18895 SW Kemmer Road, Beaverton, OR

GETTING THERE: From US 26 S, take exit 69A for Highway 217 S. From Highway 217, take the Scholls Ferry Road exit and head west. Turn right onto SW 175th and go 1.8 miles. Turn left onto SW Kemmer Road, and look for the park entrance on the left side of the road.

CONTACT: Tualatin Hills Parks and Recreation, (503) 645-6433, thprd.org; Metro, (503) 665-4995, oregonmetro.gov

WASHINGTON COUNTY

<u>72</u> BROWN'S FERRY PARK

Tualatin, 13 miles south of downtown Portland

Amble beside the Tualatin River near a historic ferry operation, and find a connection to a new greenway path.

TRAIL	Up to 2.2 miles
STEEPNESS	Gentle
OTHER USES	Bicycles
DOGS	On leash
CONNECTING TRAILS	Tualatin River Greenway Trail
PARK AMENITIES	Restrooms, kayak rentals, interpretive displays
DISABLED ACCESS	Yes

Bounded by the Tualatin River, Brown's Ferry Park, a 28-acre open space owned by the City of Tualatin, occupies the site of a pioneer-era ferry operation. Park trails travel east along the river, visiting a native tallgrass prairie, a duck pond, and a sleeve of forested wetlands. The park features a public canoe launch and an onsite boat-rental center, and flotillas of hand-powered crafts still ply the river. The park also provides a link to the newly minted 0.75-mile section of the Tualatin River Greenway Trail, which provides surprisingly peaceful passage beneath I-5 to downtown Tualatin.

A weathered brown barn marks the start of the park's trails, and wooden interpretive columns lead across Nyberg Creek to a large central pond fronted by a prairie alive with camas, yarrow, iris, and western columbine twinkling between yellow grasses. Past the pond, a narrow dirt trail edges the river to enter a forest with a small spring-fed pond shaded by big-leaf

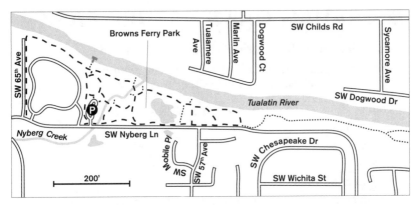

maples, firs, ash, and Pacific ninebark, and empties out at about 0.5 mile near an angular-roofed shelter. To the left, a wide paved course (officially part of the Tualatin River Greenway Trail) continues for 0.5 mile into the forest, or you can loop right to the opposite side of the pond along SW Nyberg Lane.

To find the Tualatin River Greenway Trail addition, follow the wooden walkway to the left of the canoe launch for 0.2 mile, turning up a sidewalk to meet SW Nyberg Lane. Turn right to connect to SW Nyberg Street, and head right on a sidewalk to the Nyberg Woods shopping center. The trail starts again 0.3 mile ahead, at the corner of the parking lot. Opened in spring 2016, this portion drops down to border the river on cedar boardwalks and smooth pavement with nifty displays detailing the Ice Age Missoula Floods, complete with replica mammoth tusks and footprints.

ADDRESS: 5855 SW Nyberg Lane, Tualatin, OR

GETTING THERE: From I-5 S take exit 289 for SW Nyberg Street and turn left. Go 0.3 mile, turn left onto SW Nyberg Lane, and look for the park on the left.

CONTACT: Tualatin Parks and Recreation, (503) 691-3061, www.tualatinoregon .gov/recreation

<u>73</u> GRAHAM OAKS NATURE PARK

Wilsonville, 20 miles south of downtown Portland

Modern innovation and a connection to ancient cultures make Graham Oaks Nature Park a fascinating destination.

TRAIL	Up to 3 miles; 2.2 miles as described here
STEEPNESS	Gentle
OTHER USES	Bicycles on Ice Age Tonquin Trail
DOGS	Ice Age Tonquin Trail only
CONNECTING TRAILS	Ice Age Tonquin Trail
PARK AMENITIES	Restrooms, interpretive displays, picnic shelters
DISABLED ACCESS	Yes

Opened in 2010 by Metro, Graham Oaks Nature Park in Wilsonville is loaded with modern-day urban nature park touches. The wide entrance plaza is outfitted with bioswales to reduce runoff. Shelters boast eco roofs and recycled-plastic construction. A solar-powered park restroom feeds power to the grid. You can even download an MP3 of an audio walking tour. Yet the underlying goal is to jettison park-goers into the past—back to an oak savanna landscape that might be more recognizable to ancient Kalapooias.

For millennia, native peoples tended the southern Willamette Valley's prairies (of which only about 1 percent remain) with well-honed methods like burning grasses and thinning small trees to help maintain oaks, which provided a year-round food source in the form of acorns. Since 2007, intensive restoration efforts—including planting a jaw-dropping 100 million grass and flower seeds as well as 150,000 trees, such as oaks and pines—have attempted to turn back the clock.

The wide Ice Age Tonquin Trail (a regional connector trail that planners hope

will link Sherwood, Tualatin, and Portland) threads north and south through the middle the park, providing the backbone of a 2-mile loop option that ranges from deep conifer forest to open prairies and pockets of wetlands.

From the main trailhead, you can follow the Ice Age Tonquin Trail to the 0.4-mile Legacy Creek Trail, where a cool forest of Douglas

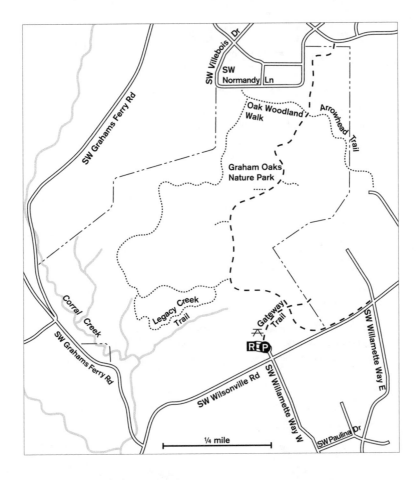

firs—some estimated at 700 years old—envelops walkers, revealing a deep ravine and creeks below. The Coyote Way Trail connects to the Legacy Creek Trail and makes a wide loop north for nearly a mile, touring a prairie setting with oaks and pines planted in uneven rows that mimic natural growth patterns. Looping back to the Ice Age Tonquin Trail, you'll visit a small stone plaza with an epic shade tree—the Elder Oak, a solitary 200-year-old Oregon white oak with a sprawling city of limbs rising above native grasses.

ADDRESS: 11825 SW Wilsonville Road, Wilsonville, OR

GETTING THERE: From I-5 S, take exit 283 for SW Wilsonville Road. Turn right onto SW Wilsonville Road and look for the trailhead on the right.

CONTACT: Metro, (503) 665-4995, oregonmetro.gov

74 JACKSON BOTTOM WETLANDS PRESERVE

Hillsboro, 24 miles west of downtown Portland

A pair of short loop options visits the heart of a 725-acre Hillsboro wildlife refuge along the Tualatin River.

TRAIL	Up to 4.5 miles
STEEPNESS	Gentle
OTHER USES	Pedestrians only
DOGS	Not allowed
CONNECTING TRAILS	None
PARK AMENITIES	Visitor center, nature walks, interpretive displays
DISABLED ACCESS	None

You may never walk the same route at Jackson Bottom Wetlands Preserve. Set in the low-lying basin beside the Tualatin River, portions of the trails are often submerged for much of the rainy season, necessitating detours. Tracts of paths

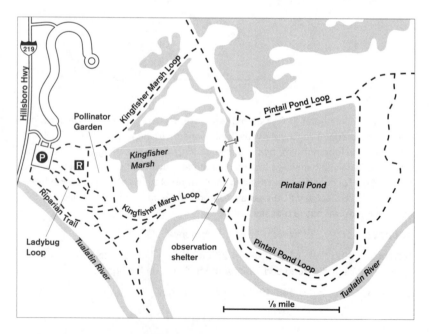

are also closed seasonally due to nesting birds like ospreys and herons. The constant state of change is unlikely to trip you up though, because there's always something new to appreciate at this 725-acre Hillsboro gem.

Trails fan out behind the visitor center, which sits on a slight ridge above the refuge. A large covered viewing shelter next to a 2-acre pollinator garden provides a good overlook before dropping down to the trails. The most popular options are a pair of roughly 0.5-mile loops around Kingfisher Marsh and the adjacent Pintail Pond just to the east, behind the marsh.

The marsh loop rounds a lower basin with a small slough that's filled with tall grasses, and offers a good chance to see red-winged blackbirds, western scrub jays, or even a belted kingfisher. At the northeast edge of the marsh, just beyond birdhouses claimed by chattering tree swallows, you can stroll up an earthen ramp to a dike to start the loop around Pintail Pond, which in winter is an aquatic landing pad for scads of tundra swans and seems to host a perennial selection of geese and ducks. In the spring of 2016, a pair of nesting ospreys took up residence at the south end of the pond, so look for periodic closures for this portion of trail.

Toward the opposite edge of the pond, a spur trail leads out along an open field bordered by black cottonwoods and Oregon ash to a secluded wetland that is home to a large heron rookery. Plan a stop in the visitor center museum to see a salvaged eagle nest (recovered from nearby Fernhill Wetlands—see Walk #75). Measuring 8 feet deep and 6 feet wide, it's thought to be the only one of its kind on display in the nation.

ADDRESS: 2600 SW Hillsboro Highway, Hillsboro, OR

GETTING THERE: From US 26 W, take exit 57 for Glencoe Road. Head south for 6 miles, passing through downtown Hillsboro. Glencoe becomes First Avenue and then SW Hillsboro Highway (OR 219). Look for the entrance on the left.

CONTACT: Hillsboro Parks and Recreation, (503) 681-6206, hillsboro-oregon.gov

WASHINGTON COUNTY

75 FERNHILL WETLANDS

Forest Grove, 27 miles west of downtown Portland

Enjoy a cornucopia of observable birdlife along a flat 1-mile loop path circling newly restored water-treatment ponds.

TRAIL	1.1-mile loop
STEEPNESS	Gentle
OTHER USES	Pedestrians only
DOGS	Not allowed
CONNECTING TRAILS	None
PARK AMENITIES	Group picnic shelter, restrooms, interpretive signs
DISABLED ACCESS	Yes

Managed by Clean Water Services along with the City of Forest Grove, this 700-acre wetland area near the Tualatin River has long been considered a jewel for birders—and things just keep getting better. A new ADA-compliant crushed-gravel path opened in 2015 accesses a water garden designed by Hoichi Kurisu, a noted Oregon landscape architect who specializes in healing gardens. Throughout  about 90 acres' worth of ponds, 750,000 native plants have taken root alongside 180 bird-attracting snags anchored into place. For the treatment plant, the increased restoration work is an innovative effort to naturally filter and cool water before it is released into the river. For birds it's a heyday.

Fernhill has a log of about two hundred different bird species that frequent the area, including nesting pairs of bald eagles, peregrine falcons, hawks, and owls, as well as shorebirds like long-billed dowitchers and sandpipers. Geese arrive by the thousands in the winter. And seeing them doesn't get much easier.

The main 1.1-mile loop is essentially a wide-open dirt road that passes around a large treatment pond, with access to another smaller neighboring pond. Loops are possible in either direction, but to see the new water-garden area, follow the crushed-gravel path just to the left of the parking lot. A row of landscaped boulders leads to a pair of spiffy arched bridges hewn from Douglas firs that provide

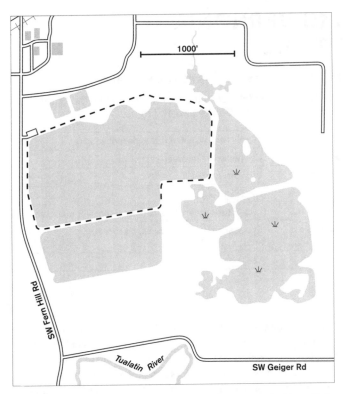

an elevated view of the pond. Past the bridge, a wood-chip path turns left to a marsh lined with birdhouses and a small viewing platform.

Sticking to the main loop, you'll pass along a dike leading to a large viewing gazebo where you can examine three interconnected wetland areas to the east and the main pond to the west. Bald eagles are often spotted from this water-bound corner. As you continue around the loop, another viewing structure provides a chance to furtively observe the growing catalog of birds before you head back to the trailhead.

ADDRESS: 1399 SW Fern Hill Road, Forest Grove, OR

GETTING THERE: From US 26 W, take exit 57 for NW Glencoe Road and head south. Turn right onto NW Zion Church Road, which becomes NW Cornelius Schefflin Road. At a roundabout, turn right onto NW Verboort Road. Go 0.4 mile, and head right on NW Martin Road at the next roundabout. Go 1.9 miles and turn left onto OR 47. Continue 1.1 miles and turn left onto SW Fern Hill Road and into the parking lot.

CONTACT: Clean Water Services, (503) 681-3600, fernhillnts.org

76 BANKS-VERNONIA STATE TRAIL

Buxton, 31 miles northwest of downtown Portland

Explore a prime walking section of this 21-mile 2016 Rail-Trail Hall of Fame nominee connecting Banks and Vernonia.

TRAIL	21 miles one way; 6 miles as described here
STEEPNESS	Gentle (with one steep section)
OTHER USES	Bicycles, horses
DOGS	On leash
CONNECTING TRAILS	L. L. "Stub" Stewart State Park, Caddywhomper Way
PARK AMENITIES	Group shelter, picnic tables, pit toilet, interpretive signs
DISABLED ACCESS	Yes

There are about as many ways to walk the Banks-Vernonia State Trail as there are miles to walk. Famous as Oregon's first rail-to-trail project, this immaculate path stretches 21 paved (and car-free) miles from Banks to Vernonia in the foothills of the Coast Range west of Portland. Access points can be found at either end of the trail in its namesake towns—Banks in the south, Vernonia in the north—and at five junctions in between, including L. L. "Stub" Stewart State Park, located at the trail's midpoint.

For sheer walking pleasure, it's tough to beat an outing from the Buxton Trailhead, set just south of the trail's 7-mile mark. (Mile markers count up from the Banks Trailhead.) Here you'll visit the Buxton Trestle, an enormous historic railroad span open to trail users, and then amble within the quiet forests of L. L. "Stub" Stewart State Park.

For a fun view of the bridge, follow the equestrian bypass trail to the left of the parking lot. The path dips steeply into a basin and crosses pretty Mendenhall Creek. Overhead the trestle soars.

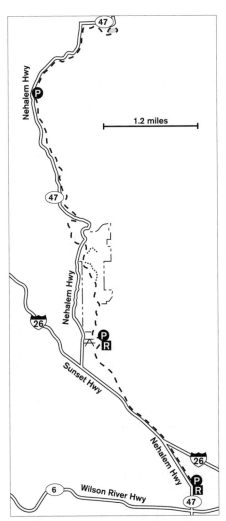

1.2 miles

Built in 1920 (and now retrofitted with a new deck and guardrail), the trestle is a mass of interconnected wooden beams that towers 80 feet high and spans 735 feet in a graceful curve above the valley floor. Atop the bridge, birds dart by at eye level, and Coast Range treetops and barn-dotted fields are visible in the distance.

At the north end of the trestle, follow a corridor of Douglas firs across Bacona Road. Over the next mile, the path climbs gently into 1,800-acre L. L. "Stub" Stewart State Park. Filled with a profusion of young alders, maples, ash, and other deciduous trees, this section is ideal for autumn tours. Just past mile marker 8, you can detour to the state park's Caddywhomper Way trail for a 1-mile trek up an old logging road that rises steeply to a hilltop meadow and overlook.

For a good turnaround point on the Banks-Vernonia State Trail, head about 0.5 mile beyond the Caddywhomper Way spur to an interpretive panel that stands over a deep ravine, marking where another massive logging trestle once stood.

ADDRESS: Bacona Road north of NW Fisher Road, Buxton, OR

GETTING THERE: From US 26 W and 217, drive about 23 miles and turn right onto NW Fisher Road. Go approximately 0.5 mile, continuing through Buxton. The road becomes Bacona Road. Bear right and look for the trailhead on the right.

CONTACT: Oregon State Parks, (503) 324-0606, oregonstateparks.org

<u>77</u> CHAMPOEG STATE HERITAGE AREA

Wilsonville, 22 miles southwest of downtown Portland

Discover the roots of Oregon's government as you walk the banks of the Willamette River in this 615-acre state park.

TRAIL	Up to 3.9 miles
STEEPNESS	Level to gentle
OTHER USES	Bicycles
DOGS	On leash
CONNECTING TRAILS	None
PARK AMENITIES	Visitor center, interpretive museum, restrooms, campground, disc-golf course
DISABLED ACCESS	Yes

So how *do* you say *Champoeg*? Most locals agree on "Sham-*poo*-ee." (Previously thought to be French, the word is now believed to stem from a Kalapooian term for an edible root.) This much is certain: Champoeg had big dreams. In 1843 Oregon's provisional government formed here. A booming steamboat hub followed. Some dreamed of Champoeg rivaling San Francisco. It didn't last. Set on the banks of the Willamette River, the settlement washed away in an epic flood in 1861.

The blank slate of a field that remains now forms the core of a popular 615-acre state park brimming with historical character. Take in the exhibit-packed museum inside the barn-themed visitor center (which sits on a bluff above the floodplain) and inspect a preserved homestead barn. Steps lead down to the main park road, where a paved bike path links day-use areas divided by the prairie.

Head right (east) for a 0.8-mile walk through the Oak Grove day-use area, past a not-so-historic disc-golf course, to reach the Kitty Newell Trail. Named for the matriarch of a prominent pioneer family, this short loop occupies parts of an old wagon road and offers multiple Willamette River overlooks near the Newell gravesite along Champoeg Creek.

At the eastern edge of the Oak Grove day-use area, the wood-chip Townsite Trail tracks west along the river for 1 mile. Nesting boxes for rare western blue-birds have been placed along this stretch, which passes large maples, cotton-woods, and firs to reach the original townsite. Wooden street posts are the only markers of where the settlement stood.

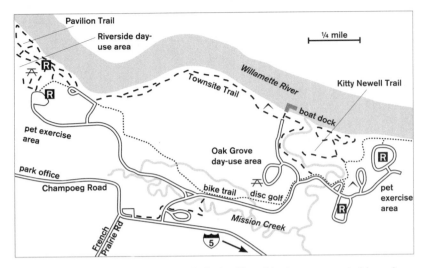

At the west end of the Townsite Trail, the Riverside day-use area holds a pioneer cabin museum and a stone monument to the provisional government. To loop back to the visitor center, follow the blacktop 0.6 mile along the southern edge of the field. Keep an eye out for a pair of boards noting flood crests—a board marking the 1996 water level is bolted to a thick black locust at knee level. A board indicating the 1861 water level hangs about 7 feet above.

ADDRESS: 7679 Champoeg Road NE, Saint Paul, OR

GETTING THERE: From I-5 S, take exit 282A and continue onto Portland-Hubbard Highway. Go 1 mile and turn right onto Arndt Road. Go 3.5 miles and turn left onto 2nd Street/Butteville Road. Go 0.5 mile, turn right onto Champoeg Road, and look for the park entrance on the right. A $5 day pass is required.

CONTACT: Oregon State Parks, (503) 678-1251, oregonstateparks.org

ACKNOWLEDGMENTS

This first edition of *Take a Walk: Portland* marks a new chapter for me and for Sasquatch Books. As this is my first guidebook project, I put my heart (and my soles) into everything that's here. I hope that it serves users faithfully, and I thank you for reading. There's simply no way I could have completed this project without the support and encouragement of my wife, Elizabeth. She is truly my better half. I can never say thanks enough for her understanding when I disappeared for hours on end to check out another trail and for always leaving a light on for me when I was out late. A big thank-you also goes to my brother, John, who abandoned his own family in Texas to accompany me on a week of soggy early spring walks in the Northwest. I won't soon forget our time on the trails. Lastly, thank you to Gary Luke and Sasquatch Books for reaching out to me for this project. It's been a privilege. May there be many more editions.

INDEX OF PARKS
AND WALKS

Wilderness Park (Walk #61)

ABOUT THE AUTHOR

Brian Barker is a contributing editor with *Portland Monthly* and has written the magazine's Trail of the Month and Field Notes columns for nearly a decade.